ROTARY HEIRLOOM QUILTS

NANCY BRENAN DANIEL

American Quilter's Society

P. O. Box 3290 • Paducah, KY 42002-3290
www.AQSquilt.com

D1279208

Located in Paducah, Kentucky, the American Quilter's Society (AQS) is dedicated to promoting the accomplishments of today's quilters. Through its publications and events, AQS strives to honor today's quiltmakers and their work and to inspire future creativity and innovation in quiltmaking.

EDITOR: JANE TOWNSWICK
TECHNICAL EDITOR: HELEN SQUIRE
GRAPHIC DESIGN: LYNDA SMITH
COVER DESIGN: MICHAEL BUCKINGHAM
PHOTOGRAPHY: CHARLES R. LYNCH

Library of Congress Cataloging-in-Publication Data

Daniel, Nancy Brenan.
    Rotary heirloom quilts / by Nancy Brenan Daniel.
        p.   cm.
    ISBN 1-57432-800-X
    1. Quilting--Patterns. 2. Patchwork--Patterns. 3. Rotary cutting.
I. American Quilter's Society II. Title

TT835 .D355 2002
746.46'041--dc21
            2002015285

Additional copies of this book may be ordered from the American Quilter's Society, PO Box 3290, Paducah, KY 42002-3290, or online at www.AQSquilt.com.

CONTENTS

DELECTABLE MOUNTAINS
page 32

ACKNOWLEDGMENTS

Every author and designer of quilts believes they can turn in a perfect manuscript, but we know that isn't true. It takes more talents than we possess to refine the material, check our math and measurements, and create the beautiful illustrations that will bring the quilts and the book to life.

I thank Barbara Smith, executive editor at the American Quilter's Society, for thinking my original material had merit, and extend my gratitude also to the many special people at AQS who shared their talents in creating the book you have in your hands. A very special thank you goes to my editor, Jane Townswick, who checked and rechecked each figure and worked hard to translate my teacher's voice into readable instructions. She seemed to know when to bend to my wishes and thoughts and when to hold fast to what she knew would make this a better book.

I was lucky to have a group of hand and machine quilters who helped with some of the sample quilts. The University Presbyterian Church Quilters, of Tempe, AZ, hand quilted the cover quilt, BUNKHOUSE SCRAPS and ALMOST AMISH. Martha Vincent of Sulphur, LA, machine quilted STARS & SPINNERS and FOUR-PATCH & NINE-PATCH. Quilting Keepsakes of Flagstaff, AZ, machine quilted the DELECTABLE MOUNTAINS. Ellen Addington of Phoenix, AZ, and I machine quilted FOLKLORIC.

Without exaggerating, I have had thousands of students over the years, and they have taught me a great deal. They have shared their talents and questions with me. My gratitude is enormous.

INTRODUCTION

My primary purpose in writing this book is to provide a variety of elegant new and treasured old heirloom quilt patterns to make quickly and easily, using rotary cutting and quick piecing techniques – quilts you can enjoy making, display in your home, or give away with pride to special friends or loved ones. Some time ago, quick-piecing pioneers Barbara Johannah, Blanche and Helen Young, Donna Poster, and Anita Hallock among others, devised inventive and ingenious methods of sewing rotary-cut strips or units together, and re-cutting them to create various patchwork units and sewing the units back together to create beautiful quilt blocks. My goal in creating the projects in this book is to share what I have learned from these talented quiltmakers and add some of my own insights and innovations to the current rotary-cutting lexicon.

The secondary purpose of this book is to offer some advice and easy-to-use tips and tricks about color that you can apply to any of your quilt projects.

Each project features its own set of rotary cutting and quick-piecing techniques, including the "stitch-and-flip" method I like for using squares to add triangles to patchwork pieces or units, and a technique I have developed, which I call "feathered patchwork." This technique is unique, in that you can sew triangles and wedge shapes together in a long strip, rotary cut the strip into narrower segments, rearrange and re-sew the segments into an intricate-looking design that takes a minimum of effort. You can see this technique in the DELECTABLE MOUNTAINS quilt on page 32, as well as in BUNKHOUSE SCRAPS on page 56, and FEATHERED CLOUDS & FLYING GEESE on page 60. Each project also includes innovative tips on color, or hints for making exciting scrap quilts from the various patterns.

This is a book for quilters who are experienced at rotary cutting and machine piecing, feel comfortable interpreting a variety of rotary-cutting diagrams, and can carry out standard finishing techniques on their own. For that reason, only basic guidelines are provided for machine piecing, rotary-cutting, and finishing. If you would like more information on any of these topics before beginning to make one of the projects in this book, refer to the Bibliography on page 94 or your favorite books on basic quiltmaking skills.

Within the following pages, I hope you will find graceful designs that are as modern as tomorrow, as traditional as yesterday, and all easier to make than ever before.

Happy quilting!

Nancy Brenan Daniel

MORRIS GARDEN
page 74

TIMESAVING TECHNIQUES

The quilts in this book are designed for rotary cutting and quick piecing. Sewing strips, triangles, squares, rectangles, and other shapes together and cutting them into patchwork segments will allow you to make each of these heirloom quilts quickly and easily. Some of the shapes, such as wedges, will need to be rotary cut from dimensions listed on diagrams, or from templates provided in the project instructions. Below, you will find lists of general sewing supplies and rotary-cutting equipment you will need to make the quilts on the following pages, along with some of my favorite tips and hints for rotary-cutting and machine-piecing success.

Sewing Supplies

Sewing machine
Use a sewing machine that has a straight-stitch capability for all machine piecing.

Machine needles
Use a quilting or sharp embroidery machine needle for machine piecing. Change the needle in your machine after approximately 4 to 6 hours of sewing time.

Threads
Use high quality, 100% cotton or cotton-covered polyester all-purpose threads for machine piecing.

Seam ripper
Use a sharp seam ripper with a safety tip for removing seams.

Fabric scissors
Use sharp scissors for trimming seam allowances and clipping threads.

Marking tools
Light and dark removable fabric markers make it easy to see lines on almost any fabric. Experiment with scraps of fabric you plan to use in your quilt to determine which marking tools you like best.

Rotary Cutting Equipment

Rotary Cutters
Choose a rotary cutter that is comfortable and designed to be used in your dominant hand. There are now good tools designed for both right-handed and left-handed people. If you are ambidextrous, look for a rotary cutter that can be used in either hand. I like to keep one at my cutting table and one beside me at my sewing machine.

Blades
Sharp rotary-cutting blades make the cutting process a much more pleasurable experience. Dull blades result in gnawed, uneven edges (and frustrated quilters)! Change the blade in your rotary cutter often, and discard used blades safely, so that no one can be accidentally injured by them.

Cutting Mats
My favorite rotary mat size is 24" x 36", with a marked grid on one side. I use a self-healing mat, because I believe the fabric clings to this type better. Consider purchasing more than one cutting mat; I own several that I use next to my sewing machine and take with me when I travel.

Acrylic Rulers
Look for accurate measurements that are easy to read on rotary rulers of any shape or size. For starters, select a 6" x 24" straight ruler and another ruler that measures 6" x 12". Look for rulers with marked lines indicating 45° and 60° angles, which can be used for cutting the triangles and wedge shapes in this book. Eventually you will acquire various rulers and triangles in different widths, lengths and shapes. Invest in them as you need them.

Steps to Rotary Cutting Accuracy

Preparing the fabric properly and using good rotary cutting tools will make the cutting experience more accurate and enjoyable. Follow these steps to ensure rotary cutting success, and refer to the Bibliography on page 94 for books with further information on rotary cutting.

1. Start by straightening the grain of the fabric by pulling at opposite corners. First, pull in one direction and then in the opposite direction.

2. Fold the fabric once, placing the selvage edges together. The fabric needs to be flat and smooth for accurate rotary cutting.

3. Place the folded fabric along one of the horizontal lines on the cutting mat. The grid lines are important for ensuring straight cuts. Let the fabric extend to the right if you are right-handed, or to the left if you are left-handed.

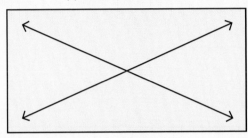

4. Lay a ruler along one of the vertical gridlines and on the horizontal line where the fold is placed. Slip the ruler over the raw edges of the fabric and realign the horizontal and vertical lines of the ruler with those on the mat. Open the rotary cutter blade, place it flush against the acrylic ruler, and press down firmly. Beginning on the mat, move the rotary cutter toward the fabric (away from you) and cut through the folded fabric with a single, clean motion. This first cut is to trim just enough of the fabric away to create a straight edge at the left side (or the right side, if you are left-handed).

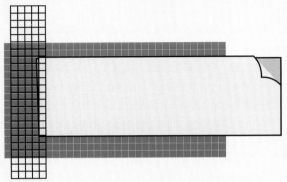

5. After trimming a straight edge, realign the fabric with the horizontal line on the mat, if necessary, and reposition ruler on the fabric at whatever strip width you wish to cut. Take note of the type and number of pieces you will need to cut for your quilt. Post this information close to your cutting table and refer to it often as you cut the pieces for your quilt. In this way, you will be more likely to cut only what you need. I'm always reminded of the carpenter's rule: "Measure twice – cut once!"

More Rotary Cutting Tips & Tricks

After you've mastered the basics of rotary cutting, remember the following tips and tricks to ensure successful rotary cutting every time.

♦ Rotary cutters perform best and stay sharp longer when used on 100% cotton fabrics.
♦ Rotary cutters will cut up to twelve layers at a time. Experiment to determine the number of layers you are able to cut with accuracy.
♦ Do not make gestures with your hand while you are holding a rotary cutter – danger may lie ahead!
♦ Always keep your cutting mat on a flat surface. When you are not using it, store it flat and away from heat, to avoid warping it.
♦ Pin a written identification label to each stack of cut strips and pieces for a quilt, including the binding strips. That way, there can be no confusion between strips or pieces of similar widths or sizes.

Machine-Piecing Guidelines

Here are some of my favorite tips and tricks for ensuring machine-piecing accuracy.

Know your sewing machine. Before making any of the quilts in this book, take a minute to sew two scrap strips of fabric together to make sure that you are stitching an accurate ¼" seam allowance. Precise stitching is critical for making sure that your finished quilts will be the correct size. Inaccurate seam allowances can cause significant problems.

For example, a mere ¹⁄₁₆" error repeated over eight seam allowances can equal a 1" change in the finished dimensions of a quilt. I use one of two European-made sewing machines, one of which produces a generous ¼" seam allowance, while the other sews a scant ¼" seam allowance. It is best to always start and finish any quilt on the same sewing machine and be as accurate as possible with the width of your seam allowances throughout the entire project.

Know your own sewing habits. If you find that your seam allowance width is inconsistent, analyze the way you sit at your sewing machine and how it affects your piecing. For example, I tend to tip my head to one side as I sew, which can lead to slight variations in seam allowance widths. Becoming aware of your posture and personal sewing habits can help you make your machine piecing more accurate.

Sew all patchwork seam allowances with the right sides of the fabric together unless otherwise stated in the project instructions.

Press all seam allowances to one side and toward the darker fabric, unless otherwise indicated in the project instructions

Sew border strips and binding strips together with diagonal seams. Trim the excess fabric on the wrong side to ¼" from your stitching lines. Press these seam allowances open to avoid bulky areas in borders and bindings.

Press patchwork seam allowances on a very firm board, which will flatten the seams better than a softer surface.

To make the backing of a quilt, determine whether you want the seam(s) in the backing to be vertical or horizontal. Determine how many lengths of fabric you will need to sew together to create the backing. Trim the selvage edges before sewing the lengths of backing fabric together. Press the seam allowances open to avoid bulk in areas to be quilted.

The quilts in this book feature double-fold French binding, and the cut strip width is 2½". Refer to the Bibliography on page 94 or to your favorite book on quiltmaking techniques for instructions on how to attach double-fold French binding to a quilt.

Sewing and Rotary Cutting Terms

Chain piecing: Sewing many of one type of unit in one continuous, long chain, without lifting the presser foot or cutting thread between units.

Finger-pressing: Opening a stitched seam allowance with your fingers and pressing the seam allowance flat with the balls of your fingers, taking care not to stretch or distort the fabric.

Strip piecing: Sewing long strips of fabric to each other or to previously sewn units

Strip sets: The combination of two or more sewn strips; strip sets are then cut into smaller segments to create various units of patchwork.

Squaring blocks: Measuring and trimming pieced blocks so they will all be the same size. Do not trim ¼" seam allowances away.

USING COLOR EFFECTIVELY

Planning a Quilt:
The Importance of Color, Value, and Contrast

As Plato, the Greek philosopher, once stated, "composition consists of observing and depicting diversity within unity." As quiltmakers, we can take advantage of this concept of diversity within unity to plan beautiful quilt designs. Think of the patchwork units in a quilt as the source of unity throughout a design, and consider the unlimited number of possible color combinations as the diversity that each of us can bring to our own projects.

Appreciation and use of color and contrast are very individualistic. We each have the ability to use these elements of design with little or no formal training. Color attracts the eye and sets the mood of a quilt, but it is the contrast between lights and darks (color values) that defines the shapes in a quilt design. As you plan a quilt, think about how you want your quilt to look when it is finished, how you would like the various patchwork units of the design to flow together or be divided, and how you can use value to create a quilt that reflects your own unique preferences. Keep planning the design down to the smallest detail to create quilts that sparkle with energy and life.

Use color value, which is the lightness or darkness of a color, to determine the framework of your quilt. Start by asking yourself questions like these: In what parts of the quilt would you like to feature dark fabrics? Where should lighter values be used to highlight the design? Having a framework or "skeleton" of lights and darks, as in this TESSELLATING STARS quilt, is a great way to create an effective quilt design, even before you begin to consider the element of color itself.

TESSELLATING STARS
page 22

USING COLOR EFFECTIVELY

Create visual impact by allowing one color or value to dominate the quilt instead of spotting each color equally over the pattern design. Vary the shape, size, and even distance between the various colors, as shown in this ALMOST AMISH quilt. A quilt should appear balanced and unified. It should contain enough diversity to keep viewers interested as their eyes move across the surface of the quilt.

ALMOST AMISH
page 70

FOLKLORIC
page 84

Create areas of focus within either the individual blocks or within the whole quilt design. At the stage of planning, you might consider rendering "lost and found" edges of the pattern. Another tactic might be to include an unexpected texture or accent color, as shown in this FOLKLORIC quilt.

Non-focus color and value areas of the quilt generally contain medium-valued fabrics, having little personality of their own. These fabrics are just as important as more dominant colors or values because they provide the background that supports the dominant colors and values, as you can see in this BUNKHOUSE SCRAPS quilt. Even after color and visual texture are applied to a quilt design, the underlying skeleton of value can still be seen.

BUNKHOUSE SCRAPS
page 56

GRETCHEN'S TRUMPET VINE
page 64

More Tips on Color

Effective color use is an art rather than a science, and it is an art quilters learn and understand through experience and making quilts. You may have read a considerable amount about color theory and color harmonies on a color wheel. It is possible to earn a Ph.D. in the study of color theory, do post-graduate work on the same topic, and still find more to learn about color. The good news is that almost any color can be made to go with any other color, given the right use of value, as you can see in this GRETCHEN'S TRUMPET VINE quilt.

Here are a handful of other guidelines that will add to your success in using color effectively.

There are no *absolutes* when it comes to using color – traditional color harmonies are good starting points for combining colors, but they are not meant to be rigid rules. Be creative and have fun as you play with various combinations of colors.

Color value is more important than color. Use the lightest tints and the deepest shades you can find of your favorite colors, and your quilts will become vibrant. If you love working in blues, think of the complete range of hues available, and use every blue, from pale, icy blue, to blue-violet, navy, blueberry, aquamarine, and the

deepest other blue shades. Attempting to match all the blues in your quilt makes a dull and monotonous quilt. Using an unexpected blue will add excitement.

Make it a habit to emphasize one color or type of contrast in a quilt. Allow one color or mood to dominate the design, and let other colors and values enhance the dominant element. Remember that a small amount of a light color will balance a large amount of a darker color.

Don't try to *match* reds – red is **red**, so use a variety of textures and values in your chosen color. (See *Tessellating Stars* on page 22.)

Repeat an accent color in more than one place in a quilt. Use it in the quilt center, and/or echo it in the borders. The color complement of your dominant color makes a great accent color.

Consider the theme of your quilt when choosing a color combination. For example, red and black might not be a good color scheme for a wedding quilt, but it could be wonderful as a quilted banner in school colors.

Colors evoke certain moods and personalities. Think of some of the common phrases we use that illustrate this idea, including moody blues; sunny yellow; vivacious red; calm, green pastures; or cool, blue waters. You can use those colors to create the same moods in your quilts.

Color Value Tip

Take some time to look through your stash and sort your fabrics into piles according to values – light, medium, and dark. How many stacks of each value do you have? If you're like most quilters, you may find that many of your fabrics fall into the medium-value range. There are a couple of reasons for this. First, medium values feel "safe" to buy and use in a quilt. Second, there are more medium-value fabrics available on the market than darks and lights. Use this artist's value-scale as a guide to sorting out the fabrics you now own. If you find yourself low in any particular areas, make a point to visit your local quilt shop and scope out the latest offerings in those values.

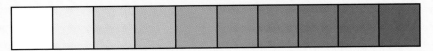

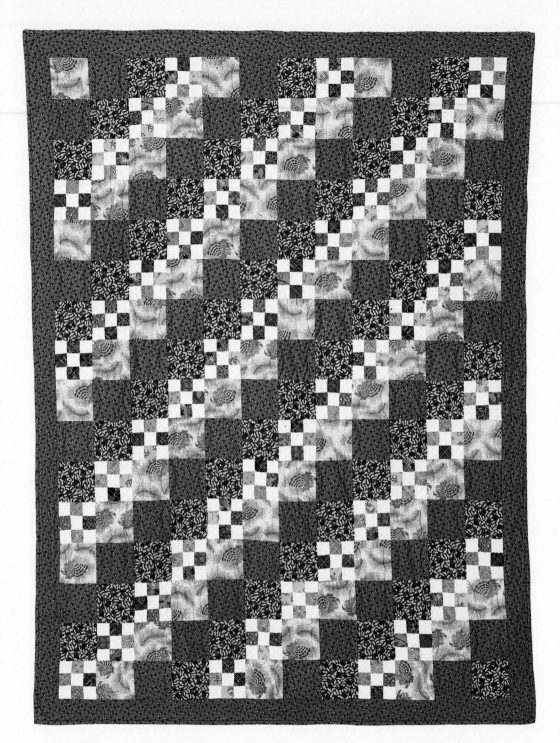

Four-Patch & Nine-Patch

Finished blocks: 3" square
Finished quilt top: 40" x 52"

The colorful Nine-Patch and Four-Patch blocks in this "Fields and Furrows" setting add up to a striking baby or lap quilt. The small spots of warm yellow, gold, and rust fabrics in the Nine-Patch blocks are a nice contrast against the blue fabrics. This scrap quilt is very easy to enlarge or reduce to any size you desire.

Fabrics and Supplies

- ⅝ yard light solid fabric for Nine-Patch blocks
- ½ yard light blue print fabric for Four-Patch blocks
- ½ yard dark blue print fabric for Four-Patch blocks
- 1¼ yards medium blue print fabric for Four-Patch blocks, border, and binding
- ⅛ yard each of 8 different fabrics in various warm colors, from dark yellow to rust
- 1¾ yards of fabric for backing
- 44" x 56" piece of batting

Cutting Fabric

FOUR-PATCH BLOCKS A AND B

From the light blue print:
- Cut four 3½" x 42" strips.

From the medium blue print:
- Cut four 3½" x 42" strips.

From the dark blue print:
- Cut four 3½" x 42" strips.

NINE-PATCH BLOCKS

From the light solid :
- Cut ten 1½" x 42" strips.

From the warm-colored:
- Cut eight 1½" x 42" strips.

BORDER AND BINDING

From the medium blue:
- Cut five 2½" x 42" strips.
- Cut five 2½" x 42" binding strips.

Piecing Four Patch Block A

1. Sew a 3½" x 42" medium blue strip to a 3½" x 42" light blue strip. Press. Make a second strip set like this one. Sew a 3½" x 42" medium blue strip to a 3½" x 42" dark blue strip. Press. Make a second set like this one.

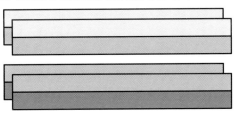

2. Cut the Step 1 strip sets into 24 segments, each 3½" wide. Sew two segment together to create Four-Patch Block A. Make 24 of Four-Patch Block A.

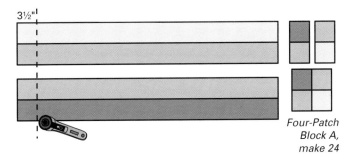

3½"

Four-Patch Block A, make 24

Piecing Four Patch Block B

3. Sew a 1½" x 42" warm-colored strip to each side of a 1½" x 42" light solid strip. Press. Make a second strip set like this one. Cut these strip sets into 48 segments, each 1½" wide.

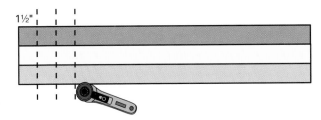

1½"

4. Sew two 1½" x 42" light solid strips to each side of a 1½" x 42" warm-colored strip. Press. Make three more strip sets like this one. Cut the four strip sets into 96 segments, each 1½" wide.

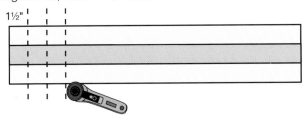

1½"

5. Sew a Step 4 segment to each side of a Step 3 segment to make a Nine-Patch Block. Press. Make 48 Nine-Patch Blocks.

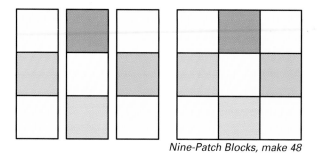

Nine-Patch Blocks, make 48

6. Sew 24 Nine-Patch Blocks to the two 3½" x 42" light blue strips. Cut the light blue fabric even with the edges of the Nine-Patch Blocks. Press the seam allowances toward the light blue fabric.

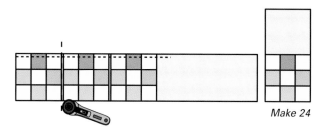

Make 24

7. Sew 24 Nine-Patch Blocks to two 3½" x 42" dark blue strips. Cut the dark blue fabric even with the edges of the Nine-Patch Blocks. Press the seam allowances toward the dark blue fabric.

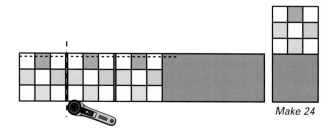

Make 24

8. Sew a Step 6 segment to a Step 7 segment to create Four-Patch Block B. Make 24 of Four-Patch Block B.

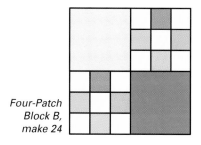

Four-Patch Block B, make 24

Assembling the Quilt Center

9. Sew the blocks together in ten rows of six blocks each, alternating the placement of Four-Patch Blocks A and B. Press the seam allowances in each row in opposite directions.

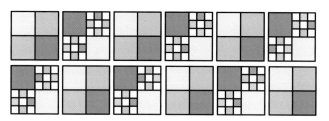

10. Referring to the previous illustration, sew the rows of blocks together, completing the quilt center. Press.

Adding the Border

11. Measure your quilt from side to side through the middle to determine the correct length for the top and bottom border strips. Trim two 2½" x 42" medium blue border strips to this measurement and sew them to the top and bottom edges of the quilt center, referring to the previous diagram. Press the seam allowances toward the border strips.

12. Measure your quilt top vertically through the middle, including the borders you just added, to determine the correct length for the side border strips. Sew the remaining 2½" x 42" border strips together, press these seam allowances open, and cut two border strips to the correct measurement. Sew these border strips to the sides of the quilt center, referring to the previous diagram. Press the seam allowances toward the border strips.

Finishing

13. Place the quilt backing wrong side up on a flat surface. Add the batting and the completed quilt top. Baste the three layers together.

14. Quilt as desired, by hand or machine.

15. Apply the binding to the edges of the quilt.

STARS & SPINNERS

Finished blocks: 6" square
Finished quilt top: 48½" x 60½"

The red and blue "spinners" at the ends of the stars may put your mind in a dizzy whirl. This pattern is actually easy to make, using two simple blocks for the center of the quilt and half-blocks to complete the spinners at the edges of the quilt.

Fabrics and Supplies

- 2 yards medium blue fabric for background
- ¼ yard each of three different light blue print fabrics for stars
- 1 yard red solid fabric for spinners and inner border
- 2 yards dark blue print fabric for spinners, outer border, and binding
- 3 yards of fabric for backing (or 2 yards of 60"-wide fabric)
54" x 66" piece of batting

Cutting Fabric

BLOCK A

From each of the three light blue:
- Cut two 2" x 42" strips.

From the medium blue background:
- Cut six 2" x 42" strips.

From the dark blue print:
- Cut four 2" x 42" strips. From these strips, cut 72 squares, each 2" x 2".

From the red solid:
- Cut four 2" x 42" strips. From these strips, cut 72 squares, each 2" x 2".

BLOCK B

From the medium blue background:
- Cut six 3½" x 42" strips. From these strips, cut 68 squares, each 3½" x 3½".

From the dark blue print:
- Cut four 2" x 42" strips. From these strips, cut 68 squares, each 2" x 2".

From the red solid:
- Cut four 2" x 42" strips. From these strips, cut 68 squares, each 2" x 2".

HALF AND CORNER BLOCKS

From the medium blue background:
- Cut five 3½" x 42" strips. From these strips, cut 52 squares, each 3½" x 3½".

From the dark blue print:
- Cut two 2" x 42" strips. From these strips, cut 24 squares, each 2" x 2".

From the red solid:
- Cut two 2" x 42" strips. From these strips, cut 24 squares, each 2" x 2".

INNER BORDER
From the red solid:
- Cut 5 strips, each 2" x 42".

OUTER BORDER AND BINDING
From the dark blue print:
- Cut 6 strips, each 5¼" x 42".
- Cut 6 strips, each 2½" x 42".

Piecing Block A

1. Sew a light blue print strip to a medium blue background strip and press. Repeat for the remaining light blue print and medium blue background strips. Cut seventy-two 3½" squares from these strip sets.

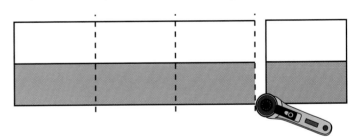

2. Place a 2" red square on one corner of the Step 1 unit, and a dark blue square at the opposite corner. Sew diagonally across these squares, as shown. Flip the triangles over and trim the excess fabric on the wrong side to a ¼" seam allowance at each corner. Press. Make a total of 72 of these units, taking care to be consistent each time you sew the 2" squares in place.

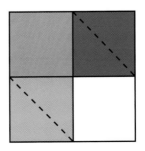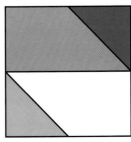

Make 72

Nancy Brenan Daniel

Rotary Heirloom Quilts

3. Sew four Step 2 units together to complete Block A. Make 18 of Block A.

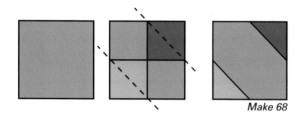

Block A, make 18

Piecing Block B

4. In the same manner, sew a 2" red square and a 2" dark blue square at opposite corners of a 3½" medium blue background square. Press. Make 68 of these units.

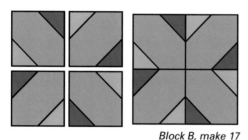

Make 68

5. Sew four Step 4 units together to complete Block B. Make 17 of Block B.

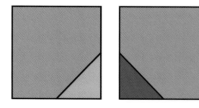

Block B, make 17

Piecing the Half Blocks

6. Sew a 2" red square to a 3½" medium blue background square and press. Sew a 2" dark blue square to a medium blue background square and press.

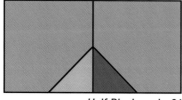

7. Sew the two Step 6 units together to complete a Half-Block. Make 24 Half-Blocks.

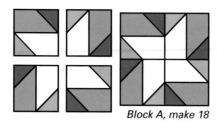

Half-Block, make 24

Assembling the Quilt Center

8. Sew three Block A's and two Block B's together, as shown and press. Make four of these rows.

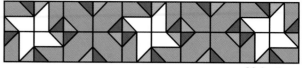

Make 4 rows

9. Sew three B blocks and two A blocks together, as shown and press three of these rows.

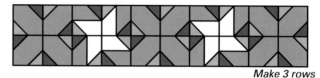

Make 3 rows

10. Sew the seven rows of blocks together, alternating them, as shown below. Press.

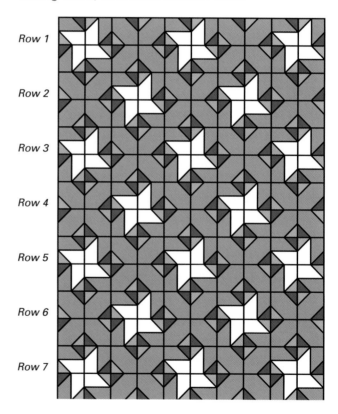

Row 1
Row 2
Row 3
Row 4
Row 5
Row 6
Row 7

Adding Corner and Half-Blocks

11. Sew five Half-Blocks together, as shown in Step #6 and #7, and press. Referring to the Quilt Assembly diagram, page 21, sew these to the top and bottom edges of the quilt, and press.

12. Sew seven Half-Blocks together, add a plain square at each end, and press. Referring to the previous diagram, sew these to the sides of the quilt and press.

Finishing

13. Referring to the Quilt Assembly diagram above, add the 2" red solid inner border strips to the quilt. Press.

14. Add the 5¼" dark blue outer border strips to the quilt. Press.

15. Place the quilt backing wrong side up on a flat surface. Add the batting and the completed quilt top. Baste the three layers together.

16. Quilt as desired, by hand or machine. Apply the binding to the edges of the quilt.

TESSELLATING STARS

Finished strip width: 1" wide
Finished quilt top: 88" x 104"

Which stars in this tessellated pattern do your eyes see first – the dark ones
or the light ones? The traditional Log Cabin method of strip sewing makes
this quilt easy to put together. Choose your favorite two colors in light and
dark values, and you can create a quilt with time-honored traditional beauty.

Fabrics and Supplies

• 6 yards total of assorted light scrap fabrics for piecing
• 10 yards total of assorted dark scrap fabrics for piecing and binding
• 7¾ yards of fabric for backing (or 3 yards of 108"-wide fabric)
• 92" x 108" piece of batting

Cutting Fabric

From the assorted light print:
• Cut strips, each 1½" wide, and as long your fabrics will allow.

From the assorted dark red:
• Cut strips, each 1½" wide, and as long your fabrics will allow. For the binding, you will need to cut 10 strips, each 2½" x 42".

Piecing Unit A

1. To start, sew two dark red 1½"-wide strips together. Press.

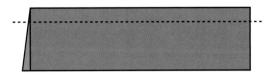

2. Cut this strip set into 1½"-wide segments. You will need a total of 154 of these segments and the ones that follow.

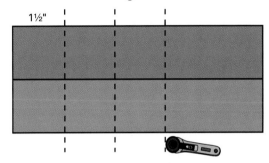

3. Sew the Step 2 units to dark 1½"-wide strips. Cut the dark strips even with the edges of the Step 2 units. Press the seam allowances toward the outside of the block.

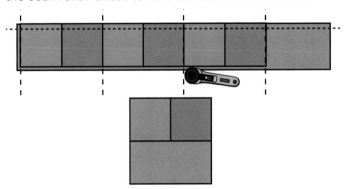

4. Sew the Step 3 units to dark 1½"-wide strips. Cut the dark strips even with the edges of the Step 2 units. Press.

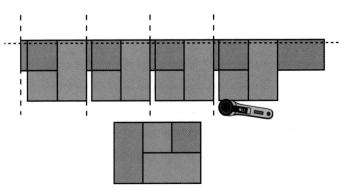

5. In the same manner, sew the Step 4 units to dark 1½"-wide strips. Cut the dark strips even with the edges of the Step 2 units. Press. Make a total of 154 of Unit A. These units measure 4½" x 4½", which includes the seam allowances.

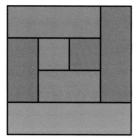

Unit A, make 154

Piecing Unit B

6. Referring to Steps 1 through 5 under "Piecing Unit A", follow the same Log Cabin strip-sewing process to make Unit B, using half dark strips and half light strips. Press. Make 22 of Unit B. These units measure 4½" x 4½", which includes the seam allowances.

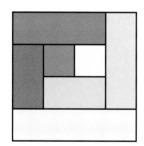

Unit B, make 22

Piecing Unit C

7. Referring to "Piecing Unit B," make 196 more of Unit B. Press. Sew the units together in groups of 4 to create Unit C, as shown below. Press. Make a total of 49 of Unit C. These units measure 8½" x 8½", which includes the seam allowances.

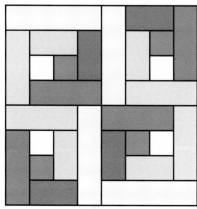

Unit C, make 49

Piecing Unit D

8. Using the Log Cabin strip-sewing process, make 20 of Unit D as shown, using assorted dark fabrics. Press. These units measure 8½" x 8½", which includes the seam allowances.

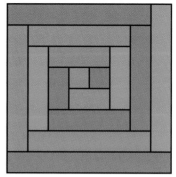

Unit D, make 20

Piecing Unit E

9. Using the Log Cabin strip-sewing process, make 30 of Unit E as shown, using assorted light fabrics. Press. These units measure 8½" x 8½", which includes the seam allowances.

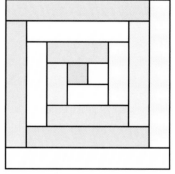

Unit E, make 30

Assembling the Quilt Top

10. Arrange the A, B, C, D, and E units in three sections, as shown on page 25. Sew the units together in rows as indicated. Press. Sew the rows together to complete each section. Press. Sew the three sections together to complete the quilt top. Press.

Finishing

11. Place the quilt backing wrong side up on a flat surface. Add the batting and the completed quilt top. Baste the three layers together.

12. Quilt as desired, by hand or machine.

13. Apply the binding to the edges of the quilt.

Section 1   Section 2   Section 3

Quilting & Assembly Tip

This large quilt was machine quilted in three sections on a standard home sewing machine. The sections were assembled and bound after the quilting process was finished.

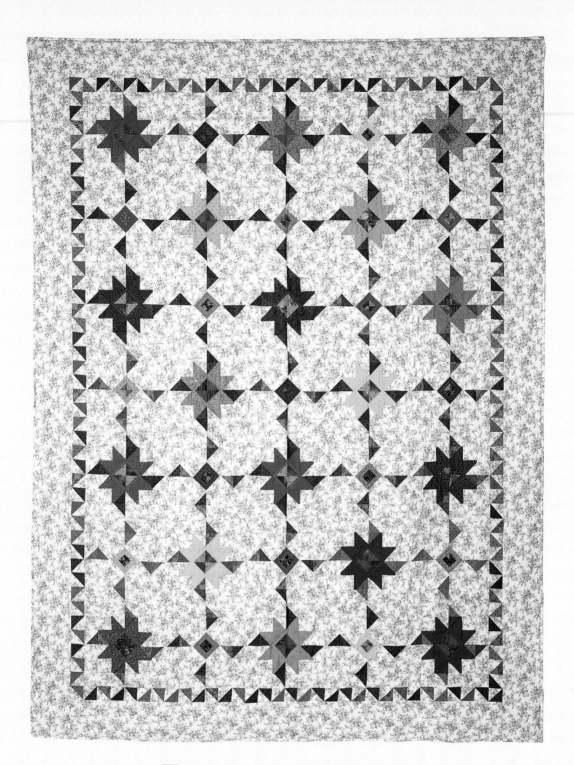

Flowers & Buds

Finished blocks: 12" square
Finished quilt top: 75" x 99"

These pieced flowers and buds will brighten up any bed. You can cut and sew them so quickly and easily, you may find yourself wanting to make more than one quilt! If inspiration strikes, consider making a dramatic variation of this design by using a very dark background fabric that will make the bright flowers shine.

Fabrics and Supplies

- 7¾ yards light print fabric for background, inner border, outer border, and binding
- 1½ yards total of assorted bright, medium, and dark print fabrics for Flower Blocks, and Bud Blocks
- ⅓ yard each of rust and dark gold print fabric for Flower and Bud centers
- 1½ yards total of assorted green print fabrics for leaves and inner border
- 5⅞ yards of fabric for backing (or 3 yards of 90"-wide fabric)
- 79" x 103" piece of batting

Cutting Fabric

FLOWER BLOCKS

From the light print:
- Cut five 2½" x 42" strips. From these strips, cut 72 squares, each 2½" x 2½".
- Cut four 2" x 42" strips. From these strips, cut 72 squares, each 2" x 2".
- Cut eight 2½" x 42" strips. From these strips, cut 72 rectangles, each 2½" x 4½".
- Cut twelve 2½" x 42" strips. From these strips, cut 72 rectangles, each 2½" x 6½".

From each of 18 assorted bright, medium, dark strips:
- Cut four rectangles 2½" x 4½" (72 total).
- Cut four squares 2½" x 2½" (72 total).

From the rust print:
- Cut three 2½" x 42" strips. From these strips, cut 36 squares, each 2½" x 2½".

From the gold print:
- Cut three 2½" x 42" strips. From these strips, cut 36 squares, each 2½" x 2½".

From the assorted green print:
- Cut seven 2" x 42" strips. From these strips, cut 144 squares, each 2" x 2".

BUD BLOCKS

From the light print:
- Cut eight 4½" x 42" strips. From these strips, cut 68 squares, each 4½" x 4½".
- Cut eight 2½" x 42" strips. From these strips, cut 68 rectangles, each 2½" x 4½".
- Cut twelve 2½" x 42" strips. From these strips, cut 68 rectangles, each 2½" x 6½".

From each of 17 assorted bright, medium, dark stripes:
- From these strips, cut 68 squares, each 2½" x 2½".

From the rust print:
- Cut two 1½" x 42" strips. From these strips, cut 34 squares, each 1½" x 1½".

From the gold print:
- Cut two 1½" x 42" strips. From these strips, cut 34 squares, each 1½" x 1½".

From the assorted green print:
- Cut seven 2" x 42" strips. From these strips, cut 136 squares, each 2" x 2".

INNER BORDER

From the light print:
- Cut six 2⅞" x 42" strips. From these strips, cut 74 squares, each 2⅞" x 2⅞". Cut these squares in half diagonally for a total of 148 triangles.

From the green:
- Cut six 2⅞" x 42" strips. From these strips, cut 74 squares, each 2⅞" x 2⅞". Cut these squares in half diagonally for a total of 148 triangles.

OUTER BORDER AND BINDING

From the light print:
- Cut ten 6" x 42" strips.
- Cut nine 2½" x 42" binding strips.

Piecing the Flower Blocks

1. Draw a diagonal line on the wrong side of all of the light print and bright, medium, and dark 2" squares. Repeat for the 2½" and 1½" rust and gold print squares. Note: This step will prepare all of these squares for both the Flower Blocks and the Bud Blocks.

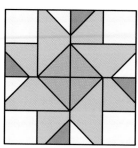

2. Arrange a 2½" light print square, a 2½" bright, medium or dark square, and a bright, medium or dark 2½" x 4½" rectangle as shown below.

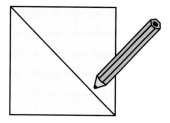

3. Sew a 2" light print square, a 2" green square, and a 2½" center square to the pieces in Step 2. Two of these center fabrics should be one color, and two should be another color. Press. Trim the excess fabric on the wrong side to a ¼" seam allowance. Sew the unit together. Make 4 of these units for one Flower Block.

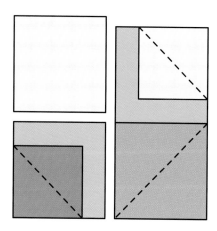

4. Sew the Step 3 units together in pairs and press. Sew the pairs of units together and press.

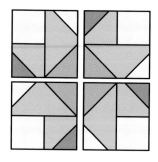

Make 18

5. Sew a 2" green square to a light print 2½" x 4½" rectangle. Press. Make another unit like this one. Sew each of these units to another light print 2½" x 4½" rectangle. Press. Sew the joined units to the top and bottom edges of the Flower Block. Sew a 2" bright, medium or dark square to a light print 2½" x 6½" rectangle. Press. Make another unit like this one. Sew each of these units to another light print 2½" x 6½" rectangle. Press. Sew the joined units to the sides of the Flower Block. Press. Repeat Steps 2 through 5 to make a total of 18 Flower Blocks.

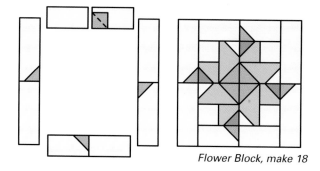

Flower Block, make 18

Piecing the Bud Blocks

6. Draw a diagonal line on all of the bright, medium or dark 1½" and 2½" squares. Sew a 2½" bright, medium or dark square to a light print 4½" square. Repeat to add another 2½" bright, medium or dark 2½" square to another light print 4½" square. Add two more 2½" bright, medium or dark squares in another color to two more light print ½" squares. Press. Trim the excess fabric on the wrong side to a ¼" seam allowance. Sew a green print 2" square to the adjacent corner of each light

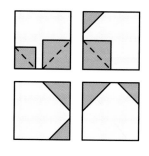

print 4½" square. Press and trim the seam allowance in the same manner. Make four of these units for each Bud Block.

7. Sew a rust or gold print 1½" square to the large triangle on each Step 6 unit. Two of these triangles should be one color, and two should be another color. Press and trim the seam allowance as before.

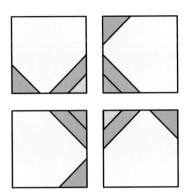

8. Sew the Step 7 units together in pairs. Press. Sew the pairs of units together. Press.

9. Sew a different green print 2" square to a light print 2½" x 4½" rectangle. Press. Make another unit like this one. Sew these units to another light print 2½" x 4½" rectangle. Press. Sew the joined units to the top and bottom edges of the Bud Block. Press.

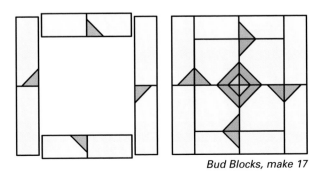

Bud Blocks, make 17

10. Sew a green print 2" square to a light print 2½" x 6½" rectangle. Press. Make another unit like this one. Sew these units to another light print 2½" x 6½" rectangle. Press. Referring to the previous diagram, sew the joined units to the sides of the Bud Block. Press.

11. Repeat Steps 6 through 10 to make a total of 17 Bud Blocks.

Assembling the Quilt Center

12. Arrange the 18 Flower Blocks and 17 Bud Blocks in seven rows of five blocks each. Sew the rows of blocks together, pressing the seam allowances in the opposite direction from row to row. Press.

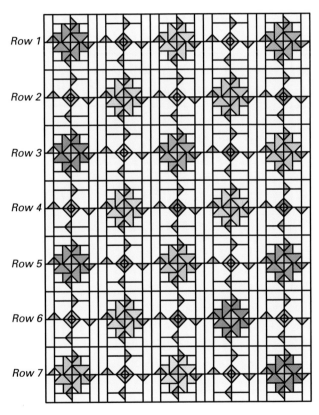

13. Referring to the diagram above, sew the seven rows of blocks together. Press.

Adding the Inner Border

14. Referring to the previous diagram, sew 148 light print 2⅞" triangles to 148 green 2⅞" triangles. Press, taking care not to distort the fabric.

15. Sew two strips of 30 half-square triangle units each. Press. Sew these border strips to the top and bottom edges of the quilt center. Press.

16. Sew two strips of 44 half-square triangles each. Press. Sew these border strips to the side edges of the quilt. Press.

Adding The Outer Border

17. Sew two light print 6" x 42" strips together and press the seam allowance open. Repeat to make another border strip like this one. Measure your quilt top from side to side through the middle to determine the correct length for the top and bottom outer border strips. Trim the two joined strips to this length, and sew them to the top and bottom edges of the quilt, referring to the Quilt Assembly diagram on page 31. Press the seam allowances toward the outer borders.

18. Sew three light print 6" x 42" strips together and press the seam allowances open. Repeat to make another border strip like this one. Measure your quilt top vertically through the center to determine the correct length for the side border strips. Trim the two joined strips to this length, and sew them to the side edges of the quilt, again referring to the Quilt Assembly diagram on page 31. Press the seam allowances toward the outer borders.

Finishing

19. Place the quilt backing wrong side up on a flat surface. Add the batting and the completed quilt top. Baste the three layers together.

20. Quilt as desired, by hand or machine.

21. Apply the binding to the edges of the quilt.

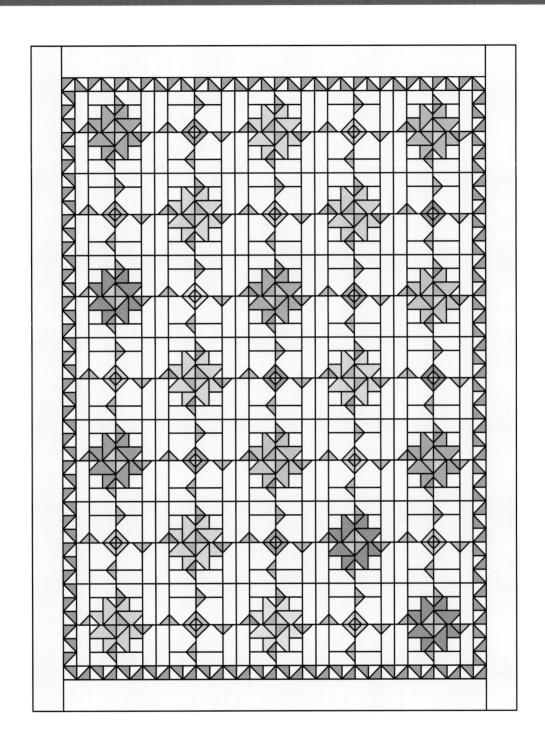

DELECTABLE MOUNTAINS

Finished block: 10" square
Finished quilt top: 90" x 90"

This version of the classic Delectable Mountains quilt is actually a series of borders surrounding an eight-pointed Star block. While the traditional method of making this quilt involves cutting and sewing many 45-degree triangles, my technique allows you to make the entire quilt without ever cutting a single triangle! By sewing large panels together and cutting the panels into narrower strips, you can rearrange the strips easily to create the angled Delectable Mountains pattern.

Fabric and Supplies

- 3 yards light solid fabric for Star block and pieced borders
- 6½ yards dark print fabric for Star block, pieced borders, inner border, outer border, and binding
- ⅔ yard of accent fabric for middle border
- 7¾ yards of fabric for backing (or 3 yards of 108"-wide fabric)
- 92" x 92" piece of batting
- 60° acrylic triangle for cutting wedge shapes
- 6" x 24" acrylic ruler for cutting strips and wedge shapes

Cutting Fabric

STAR BLOCK

From the light solid:
- Cut a 4¼" x 4¼" square. Cut this square in half diagonally in both directions.
- Cut a 3½" x 42" strip. From this strip, cut four 3½" x 3½" squares

From the dark print:
- Cut two 3" x 42" strips. From these strips, cut eight 45° diamonds, referring to page 34.

DELECTABLE MOUNTAINS PIECED BORDERS

From the light solid:
- Cut ten 7½" x 42" strips.
- Cut three 6½" x 42" strips. From these strips, cut sixteen 6½" x 6½" squares.
- Cut a 5½" x 42" strip. From this strip, cut four 5½" x 5½" squares.

From the dark print:
- Cut ten 7½" x 42" strips.
- Cut a 6½" x 42" strip. From this strip, cut four 6½" x 6½" squares.

INNER BORDER

From the dark print:
- Cut eight 2½" x 42" strips.

MIDDLE BORDER

From the accent:
- Cut eight 1½" x 42" strips.

OUTER BORDER AND BINDING

From the dark print:
- Cut ten 5½" x 42" strips.
- Cut ten 2½" x 42" binding strips.

Cutting Wedges for the Delectable Mountains Sections

1. Fold a 7½" x 42" dark print strip in half with wrong sides together and trim the selvages. Fold a 7½" x 42" strip of background fabric in half with wrong sides together and trim the selvages. Layer these folded strips.

Folds

2. Place a 60° acrylic triangle on the layered strips and cut the first edge of the wedge shape. (Or use the 60° line on a straight acrylic ruler.) Place a straight acrylic ruler and make the second cut of the wedge shape exactly 5¾" to the left of the first cut.

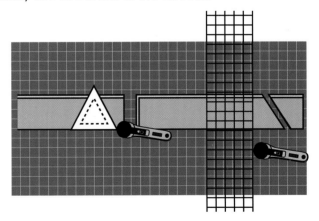

3. The finished dimensions of the wedge shapes are 7½" x 5¾" x 1½", as shown. Repeat Step 1 to cut 60 wedge shapes from the ten folded light solid strips and 60 wedge shapes from the ten folded dark print strips. This will produce mirror-image pairs.

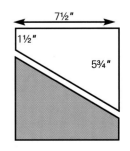

Piecing Delectable Mountains Sections

4. Sew the dark print wedge shapes to the light solid wedge shapes, offsetting the seam allowances, as shown, so that the edges of the pieced units will be straight.

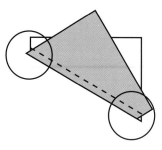

5. Make a total of 120 wedge units; 60 with the seam slanting in one direction and 60 with the seam slanting in the opposite direction, creating mirror images.

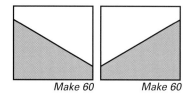

Make 60   *Make 60*

6. Cut each of the Step 5 edge units into three 2½"-wide segments.

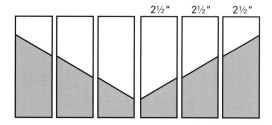

2½"   2½"   2½"

7. Rearrange the strips as shown, and sew them together into a Delectable Mountains section. Make 60 of these Delectable Mountains sections. Each section should measure 6½" x 12½"; if necessary, adjust the width of your seam allowances to make the sections the correct size. Press all seam allowances open.

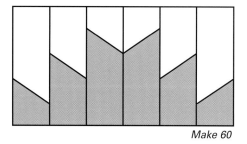

Make 60

Cutting Diamonds for the Star Block

8. Place the 45° angle line on a 6" x 24" ruler along the lower edge of a dark print 3" x 42" strip. Rotary cut along the edge of the ruler to create the first side of the diamond.

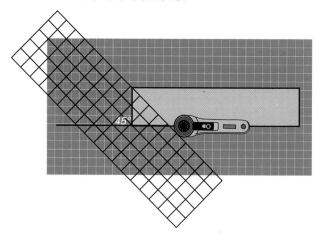

9. Move the ruler 3" to the right, keeping the 45° angle line in alignment with the lower edge of the strip. Rotary cut along the edge of the ruler to create the second side of the diamond. Cut a total of 8 diamonds for the Star Block.

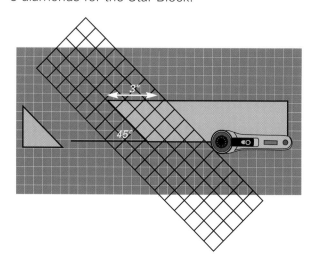

Piecing the Star Block

10. Sew two diamond shapes together, beginning and ending the seam allowance exactly ¼" in from the edge of the fabric. Sew a total of four pairs of diamond shapes. Press.

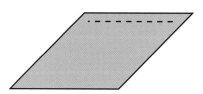

11. In the same manner, sew two pairs of diamond shapes together to create half of the star. Press. Sew the halves of the star together. Press.

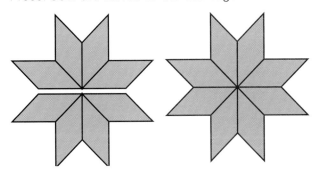

12. Pin a light solid triangle to a diamond shape, as shown below, and sew from the outer edge toward the center of the star, stopping at the point where the diamond seams meet . Pin the adjacent side of the triangle to the next diamond shape, and sew this seam in the same manner. Press. Sew the remaining three light solid triangles between the diamond shapes at the sides and bottom of the star in the same manner. Press.

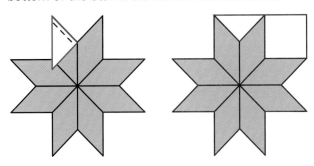

13. In the same manner, sew a 3½" light solid square at the corners of the Star Block. Press.

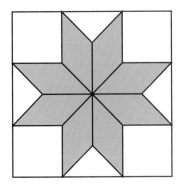

Adding Pieced Border #1

14. Sew a Delectable Mountains section to the sides of the Star Block. Press the seam allowances toward the Star block.

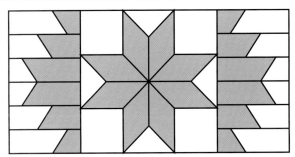

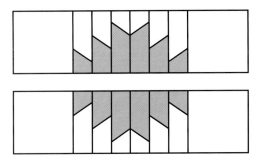

15. Sew a 6½" x 6½" light solid square to each end of two Delectable Mountains sections. Press the seam allowances toward the Delectable Mountains sections.

16. Sew the two Step 15 sections to the top and bottom edges of the Star block. Press the seam allowances toward the Delectable Mountains sections.

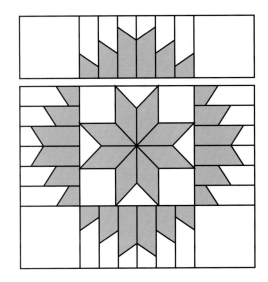

Pieced Borders #2, #3, and #4

17. Referring to the Quilt Assembly diagram on page 37, continue adding three more pieced borders in the same manner as the first, increasing the number of Delectable Mountains sections in each border as shown. Press the seam allowances in the same manner as for Pieced Border #1.

Pieced Border #5

18. Sew a light solid 5½" x 5½" square to a dark print 6½" x 6½" square diagonally from corner to corner, as shown. Open up the fabric and press, and trim the seam allowance to ¼". Make four of these corner units.

19. Assemble the Delectable Mountains sections for Pieced Border #5, referring to the Quilt Assembly diagram on the next page, and pressing the seam allowances in the same manner. Sew Pieced Border #5 to the quilt top in the same manner as for the other borders, using the Step 18 units at the corners of the last two pieced strips.

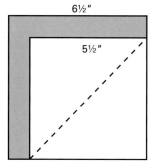
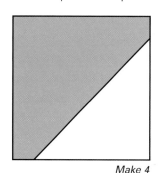

Make 4

Inner Border

20. Sew the 2½" x 42" dark print strips together, and press the seam allowances open. Measure your quilt top from side to side through the middle to determine the correct length for the top and bottom inner border strips. Cut two dark print border strips to this length, and sew them to the top and bottom edges of the quilt, again referring to the Quilt Assembly diagram. Press the seam allowances toward the border strips.

21. Measure your quilt top vertically through the middle, including the borders you just added. Cut two dark print border strips to this length and sew them to the sides of the quilt. Press the seam allowances toward the border strips.

Middle Border

22. Sew the 1½" x 42" accent strips together and press the seam allowances open. Measure your quilt top from side to side through the middle to determine the correct length for the top and bottom inner border strips. Cut two accent border strips to this length, and sew them to the top and bottom edges of the quilt, referring to the Quilt Assembly diagram on page 37. Press the seam allowances toward the border strips.

23. Measure your quilt top vertically through the middle, including the borders you just added. Cut two accent border strips to this length and sew them to the sides of the quilt. Press the seam allowances toward the border strips.

Outer Border

24. Sew the 5½" x 42" dark print strips together and press the seam allowances open. Measure your quilt top from side to side through the middle to determine the correct length for the top and bottom inner border strips. Cut two accent border strips to this length and sew them to the top and bottom edges of the quilt, again referring to the Quilt Assembly diagram on page 37. Press the seam allowances toward the border strips.

25. Measure your quilt top vertically through the middle, including the borders. Cut two dark print border strips to this length, and sew them to the sides of the quilt. Press the seam allowances toward the border strips.

Finishing

26. Place the quilt backing wrong side up on a flat surface. Add the batting and the completed quilt top. Baste the three layers together.

27. Quilt as desired, by hand or machine.

28. Apply the binding to the edges of the quilt.

Fabric and Supplies

- ¾ yard light solid fabric for Bear Paw and Maze Blocks
- ⅞ yard rose fabric for Bear Paw Block, Maze Blocks, and binding
- 29" x 29" square of fabric for backing
- 29" x 29" piece of batting

Cutting Fabric

BEAR PAW BLOCKS

From the light solid:

- Cut a 3" x 42" strip. From this strip, cut four 3" x 4¼" rectangles.
- Cut a 1¾" x 42" strip. From this strip, cut four 1¾" x 1¾" squares.
- Cut a 2⅛" x 42" strip. From this strip, cut eight 2⅛" x 2⅛" squares. Cut these squares in half diagonally.

From the rose:

- Cut a 2⅛" x 42" strip. From this strip, cut eight 2⅛" x 2⅛" squares. Cut these squares in half diagonally.
- Cut a 3" x 42" strip. From this strip, cut five 3" x 3" squares.

MAZE BLOCKS AND BINDING

From the light solid:

- Cut a 5½" x 42" strip. From this strip, cut four 5½" x 10½" rectangles.
- Cut a 6" x 42" strip. From this strip, cut four 6" x 6" squares. Cut these squares diagonally in both directions for a total of 16 triangles.

From the rose:

- Cut two 1¾" x 42" strips. From these strips, cut eight 1¾" x 10½" rectangles.
- Cut a 2½" x 42" strip. From this strip, cut four 2½" x 2½" squares.
- Cut two 2½" x 42" strips. From these strips, cut 16 pieces using Template A on page 40.
- Cut three 2" x 42" binding strips.

Piecing the Bear Paw Blocks

1. Referring to "Piecing the Bear Paw Blocks" on page 39, make one Bear Paw block using the rose and light solid fabric.

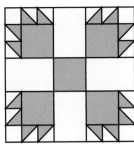

Bear Paw Block, make 1

Piecing the Maze Blocks A and B

2. Referring to "Piecing Maze Blocks A and B", steps #6-#9, and Template A on page 40, make four A and four B Maze blocks, using the rose and light solid fabrics.

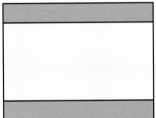 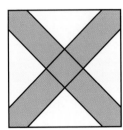

Maze Block A, make 4 *Maze Block B, make 4*

Assembling the Quilt Top

3. Referring to "Assembling the Quilt Top" and Steps #10-#13 on page 40, sew the four A and B Maze Blocks and the Bear Paw Block together.

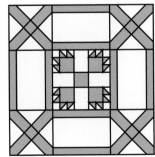

Bear Paw Medallion Quilt

Finishing

4. Place the quilt backing wrong side up on a flat surface. Add the batting and the completed quilt top. Baste the three layers together.

5. Quilt as desired, by hand or machine.

6. Apply the binding to the edges of the quilt.

MARCH PINWHEELS

Finished panels: 12" x 48"
Finished quilt top: 48" x 60"

One summer I designed and made a banner quilt that featured one lone sun-flower, very much like the central panel in this quilt. When I happened to glance at the banner one day, it made me think of a child's pinwheel toy. Because two of my children and I share March birthdays, both sunflowers and pinwheels seemed the perfect theme for making another quilt.

Fabric and Supplies

- 2¼ yards light blue variegated fabric for background
- ¾ yard dark blue print fabric for Pinwheel blocks
- ¾ yard assorted red print fabrics for flowers and buds
- 1 yard of one red print fabric for outer border and binding
- ½ yard assorted green print fabrics for stems and leaves
- ⅛ yard black print fabric for flower centers
- ⅛ yard gold print fabric for flower centers
- 3 yards of fabric for backing (or 1⅞ yards of 60"-wide fabric)
- 52" x 64" piece of batting

Cutting Fabric

FLOWER AND BUD BLOCKS

From the light blue variegated:
- Cut 5 strips, each 2½" x 42". From these strips, cut 66 squares, each 2½" x 2½".
- Cut 2 strips, each 2½" x 42". From these strips, cut 18 rectangles, each 2½" x 4½".
- Cut the remaining background fabric using the measurements on pages 47 and 48.

From the assorted red print:
- Cut 2 strips, each 2½" x 42". From these strips, cut 19 squares, each 2½" x 2½".
- Cut 2 strips, each 2½" x 42". From these strips, cut 18 rectangles, each 2½" x 4½".
- Cut 3 strips, each 2½" x 42". From these strips, cut 18 rectangles, each 2½" x 6½".

From the assorted green print:
- Cut 3 strips, each 1½" x 42". From these strips, cut 6 rectangles, each 1½" x 6½"; 2 rectangles, each 1½" x 18½"; a 1½" x 8½" rectangle; and a 1½" x 16½" rectangle.
- Cut a 2½" x 42" strip. From this strip, cut 9 squares, each 2½" x 2½".
- Cut a 2½" x 42" strip. From this strip cut 7 rectangles 2½" x 4½"; 1 rectangle 2½" x 6½".

From the black print:
- Cut a 4" x 42" strip. From this strip, cut 6 squares, each 4" x 4".

From the gold print:
- Cut a 4" x 42" strip. From this strip, cut 6 squares, each 4" Pinwheel Border and Pinwheel Blocks in quilt.

PINWHEEL BORDER AND PINWHEEL BLOCKS

From the blue variegated:
- Cut 7 strips, each 2⅞" x 42". From these strips, cut 102 squares, each 2⅞" x 2⅞". Cut these squares in half diagonally for a total of 204 triangles.

From the dark blue print:
- Cut 7 strips, each 2⅞" x 42". From these strips, cut 102 squares, each 2⅞" x 2⅞". Cut these squares in half diagonally for a total of 204 triangles.

OUTER BORDER AND BINDING

From the red print:
- Cut 6 strips, each 2½" x 42".
- Cut six 2½" x 42" binding strips.

Piecing the Flower, Bud, and Pinwheel Blocks

1. Sew six red print 2½" x 2½" squares to six blue variegated 2½" x 2½" squares. Press.

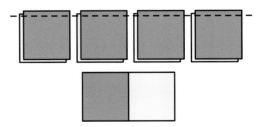

2. Sew a blue variegated 2½" x 4½" rectangle to four of the Step 1 units. Press. Reserve the two remaining Step 1 units.

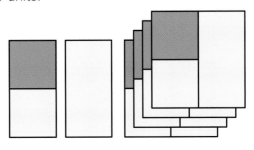

3. Sew two blue variegated 2½" x 2½" squares to each end of two green print 2½" x 4½" rectangles with diagonal seams, as shown. These leaf units must be mirror images of each other. In the same manner, sew two blue variegated 2½" x 2½" squares to the opposite ends of the green rectangles. Press and trim the excess fabric on the wrong side to a ¼" seam allowance.

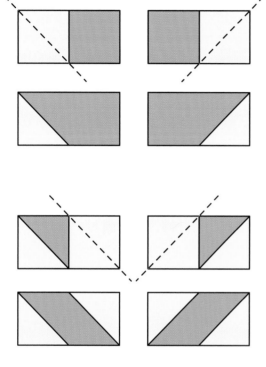

4. Sew the two Step 3 leaf units to the reserved Step 2 units.

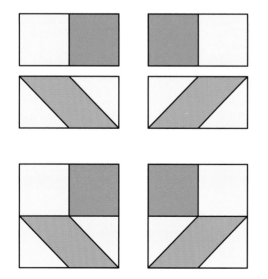

5. Sew a red print 2½" x 4½" rectangle to the two Step 3 leaf units and three of the Step 2 units.

Press. Sew a green print 2½" x 4½" rectangle to the remaining Step 2 unit. Press.

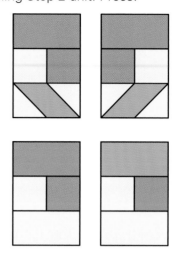

6. Sew a red print 2½" x 6½" rectangle to five of the Step 5 units. Press. Sew a green print 2½" x 6½" rectangle to the remaining Step 5 unit. Press.

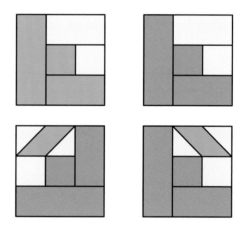

7. Sew blue variegated 2½" x 2½" squares or green print 2½" x 2½" squares to opposite corners of the Step 6 units with diagonal seams as shown. Press. Refer to the Quilt Assembly diagram on page 49 for correct color placements.

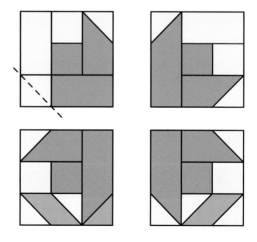

8. Sew two gold and two black 4" x 4" squares to the flower units from Step 7, using diagonal seams. Press and trim the excess fabric on the wrong side to ¼" seam allowances.

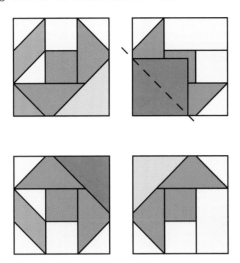

9. Chain-sew eight blue variegated 2⅞" triangles to eight dark blue print 2⅞" triangles. Press the half-square triangle units open.

10. Sew the Step 9 half-square triangle units together in pairs. Press. Sew each of the four pairs of half-square triangle units together to complete two Pinwheel Blocks. Press.

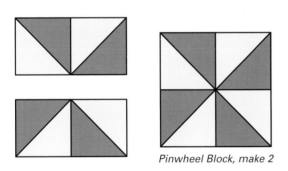

Pinwheel Block, make 2

Assembling Panels A, B & C

Refer to the individual panel diagrams (see page 48 for Panel B and Panel C) for pieced units, cut sizes, and assembly. Sew the panel together in horizontal sections, then sew the sections together to complete the panels, and press.

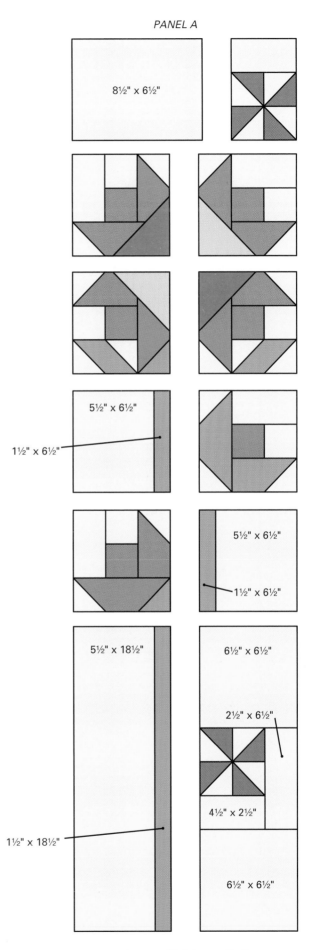

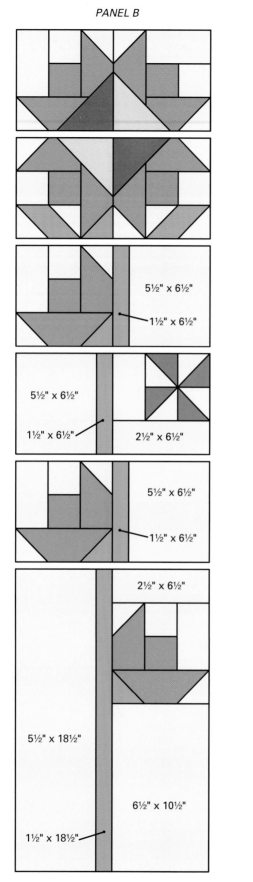

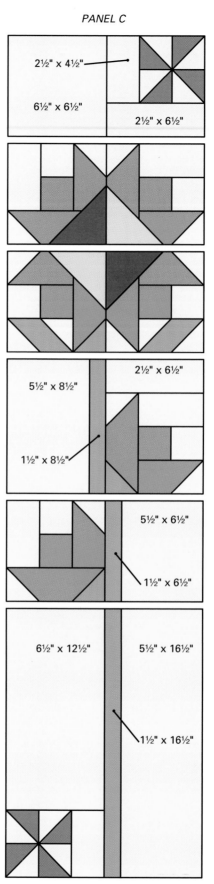

There are small variations in the number and placement of the Bud Blocks and Pinwheel Blocks in Panel B.

Note that the Pinwheel Block in the upper right corner faces the opposite direction from other Pinwheel Blocks in the quilt.

Adding the Pinwheel Border

11. Referring to Steps 9 and 10, make a total of 46 Pinwheel Blocks. Press.

Border Pinwheel Block, make 46

12. Sew nine Pinwheel Blocks together for the top and bottom border units. Press. Sew 14 Pinwheel Blocks together for each side border unit. Press. Sew these Pinwheel border units to the sides of the quilt. Press.

Adding the Outer Border

13. Measure your quilt top to determine the correct measurement for the top and bottom outer border strips. Trim two 2½"-wide red print strips to this length and sew them to the top and bottom edges of the quilt. Press the seam allowances toward the borders. Piece the remaining red print 2½" x 42" strips together in pairs. Press the seam allowances open. Measure your quilt top vertically through the middle to determine the correct measurement for the side outer border strips. Trim the pieced strips to this length and sew them to the sides of the quilt, referring to the Quilt Assembly diagram. Press the seam allowances toward the borders.

Finishing

16. Place the quilt backing wrong side up on a flat surface. Add the batting and the completed quilt top. Baste the three layers together.

17. Quilt as desired, by hand or machine. Apply the binding to the edges of the quilt.

GEOMETRIC LEAVES

Finished blocks: 6" square
Finished quilt top: 52" x 52"

Tessellated motifs fit together in a positive/negative pattern. In this quilt, the tessellation occurs in the way the large white leaves interlock with the bright and dark leaves. The small geometric leaves within several of the white leaves add a unique design element. This rich blend of oranges, reds, violets, and golds with touches of green on a light background hint at autumn's splendor. Play around with colors in your stash and look for fabrics that will allow you to interpret other seasons as well.

Fabrics and Supplies

- 2 yards light print fabric for Leaf blocks
- 1 yard total of assorted bright and dark fabrics for Leaf blocks
- ½ yard medium tan fabric for inner border
- 1½ yards total of assorted dark fabrics for outer border
- ⅓ yard dark fabric for binding
- 3¼ yards of fabric for backing (or 1¾ yards of 60"-wide fabric)
- 56" x 56" piece of batting

Cutting Fabrics

SCRAP LEAF BLOCK A (MAKE 18)

From the light print:

- Cut two 2⅞" x 42" strips. From these strips, cut 18 squares, each 2⅞" x 2⅞". Cut these squares in half diagonally for a total of 36 triangles.

From each of 18 bright or dark:

- Cut one piece using Template B, page 54.
- Cut one 2½" x 4½" rectangle.
- Cut one 2½" x 6½" rectangle.

LIGHT LEAF BLOCK B (MAKE 7)

From the light print:

- Cut seven pieces, using Template B on page 54.
- Cut a 2½" x 42" strip. From this strip, cut seven rectangles, each 2½" x 4½".
- Cut two 2½" x 42" strips. From these strips, cut seven rectangles, each 2½" x 6½".

From the bright or dark print:

- Cut seven squares, each 2⅞" x 2⅞", in colors that match the bright or dark colors in the Leaf Block A. Cut these squares in half diagonally for a total of 14 triangles.

COMBINATION LEAF BLOCK C (MAKE 11)

From the light print:

- Cut two 1½" x 42" strips. From these strips, cut 55 squares, each 1½" x 1½".
- Cut a 1⅞" x 42" strip. From this strip, cut 22 squares, each 1⅞" x 1⅞". Cut these squares in half diagonally for a total of 44 triangles.

- Cut two 2½" x 42" strips. From these strips, cut 33 squares, each 2½" x 2½".
- Cut a 2⅞" x 42" strip. From this strip, cut 11 squares, each 2⅞" x 2⅞". Cut these squares in half diagonally for a total of 22 triangles.

From each of 11 bright or dark:

- Cut one piece using Template C on page 54.
- Cut one square 1⅞" x 1⅞". Cut this square in half diagonally making two triangles.
- Cut one 1½" x 2½" rectangle.
- Cut one 1½" x 4½" rectangle.

INNER BORDER

From the light print:

- Cut a 2½" x 42" strip. From this strip, cut 12 squares, each 2½" x 2½".

From the medium print:

- Cut four 2½" x 42" strips. From these strips, cut the following: 2 rectangles, each 2½" x 4½"; 2 rectangles, each 2½" x 6½"; 2 rectangles, each 2½" x 8½"; and 8 rectangles, each 2½" x 12½".

OUTER BORDER

From the assorted dark print

- Cut 16 strips, each 2½" x 42". From these strips, cut 92 rectangles, each 2½" x 6½".

BINDING

From the dark print

- Cut 6 strips, each 2½" x 42".

Piecing Scrap Leaf Block A

1. Sew two 2⅞" light triangles to both sides of a bright or dark Template B piece. Press.

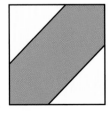

2. Sew a bright or dark 2½" x 4½" rectangle to the left side of the unit, and press. Sew a bright or dark 2½" x 6½" rectangle to the bottom of the same unit. Press. Make a total of 18 Scrap Leaf Block A.

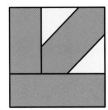

Leaf Block A, make 18

Nancy Brenan Daniel

Rotary Heirloom Quilts

Piecing Scrap Leaf Block B

3. The bright or dark colors in the triangles in Leaf Block B correspond to the placements of bright or dark colors in the Leaf Blocks A. Determine where you want to place the Leaf Block As in your quilt, and then make the Leaf Block Bs, referring to the quilt photo on page 50 for color guidance.

4. Repeat Steps 1 and 2, using 2⅞" bright or dark triangles in the appropriate colors, a light Template B piece, a light 2½" x 4½" rectangle, and a 2½" x 6½" rectangle. Make a total of seven Leaf Block Bs.

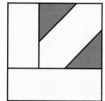

Leaf Block B, make 7

Piecing Combination Leaf Block C

5. Sew a light 1⅞" triangle to a bright or dark 1⅞" triangle. Press. Make 22 of these half-square triangle units. Sew two light 1½" squares to the left end of a half-square triangle unit and one light 1½" square to the right end. Press. Make 11 of these units.

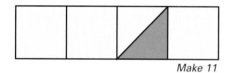

Make 11

6. Sew a light 1½" square to the left end of a bright or dark 1½" x 3½" rectangle. Press. Make 11 of these units.

Make 11

7. Sew a Step 5 half-square triangle unit to a light 1½" square. Press. Sew two light 1⅞" triangles to a bright or dark Template C piece. Press. Place a bright or dark 1½" x 2½" rectangle between the two pieced units. Sew a Step 5 unit, a Step 6 unit, and the Step 7 units together as shown.

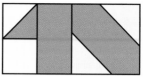

Make 11

8. Sew these three units together as shown. Press. Make 11 of these units.

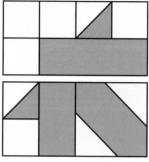

Make 11

9. Sew a light 2⅞" triangle to a bright or dark 2⅞" triangle. Make 22 of these half-square triangle units. To half of these units, sew a light 2½" square as shown. Press. To the remaining 11 units, sew two light 2½" squares as shown. Press. Sew the Step 7 unit and the Step 8 units together to complete the Combination Leaf Block C. Make a total of 11 of these blocks.

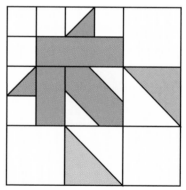

Block C, make 11

<hr/>

Color Placement

Tessellating designs can be tricky. Plan the placement of the A, B, and C Leaf Blocks in your quilt very carefully. Pin the Leaf Block As to a design wall or piece of flannel, or enlarge the quilt diagram on page 55 on a photocopy machine and paste sample fabrics in the appropriate places. Then decide which colors the triangles will need to be in the Leaf Block Bs so that they correspond to the adjacent colors in the Leaf Block As and Cs.

Assembling the Quilt Center

10. Arrange 18 Leaf Block A, seven Leaf Block B, and 11 Combination Leaf Block Cs in nine groups of four as shown below.

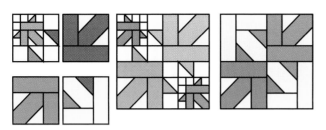

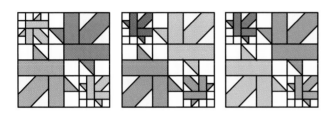

11. Sew each group of four blocks together and press. Sew the joined sections together in rows and press. Sew the rows of blocks together and press.

Adding the Inner Border

12. Sew a 2½" light square to the right end of a medium tan 2½" x 4½" rectangle with a diagonal seam. Pay careful attention to the direction of the diagonal seam. Press and trim the excess fabric on the wrong side to a ¼" seam allowance. Repeat to make another unit like this. In the same manner, sew a light 2½" square to the right end of four 2½" x 12½" rectangles, press and trim. Arrange each of these units and two 2½" x 8½" rectangles.

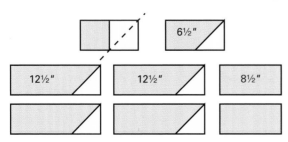

13. Sew the Step 12 units together to complete the top and bottom inner border strips. Press.

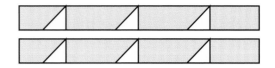

14. Sew a 2½" light square to a medium tan 2½" x 6½" rectangle with a diagonal seam, press and trim. Repeat to make another unit like this one. In the same manner, sew a 2½" light square to a medium tan 2½" x 12½" rectangle, press and trim. Make a total of four of these units.

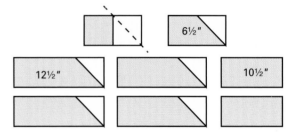

15. Sew the above units together as shown, adding a medium tan 2½" x 10½" rectangle at the right end to complete the side inner border strips. Trim the excess light fabric and press as before.

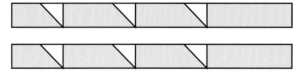

16. Sew the top and bottom inner border strips to the quilt center and press. Sew the side inner border strips to the quilt center and press.

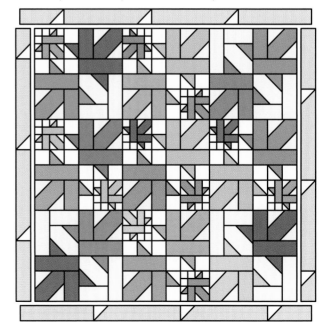

Adding the Outer Border

17. Sew 20 dark 2½" x 6½" rectangles together for the top outer border. Press. Repeat for the bottom outer border. Sew these border strips to the top and bottom edges of the quilt. Press.

18. Sew 26 dark 2½" x 6½" rectangles together for each side outer border. Press. Sew these borders to the sides of the quilt, referring to the previous diagram. Press the completed quilt top.

Finishing

19. Place the quilt backing wrong side up on a flat surface. Add the batting and the completed quilt top. Baste the three layers together.

20. Quilt as desired, by hand or machine.

21. Apply the binding to the edges of the quilt.

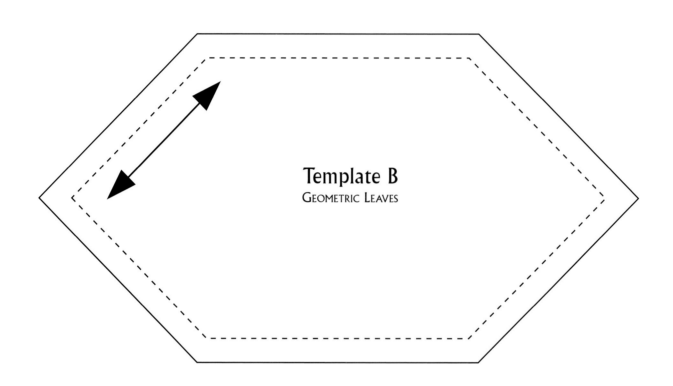

Template B
GEOMETRIC LEAVES

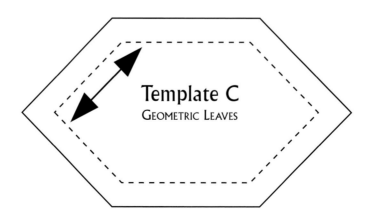

Template C
GEOMETRIC LEAVES

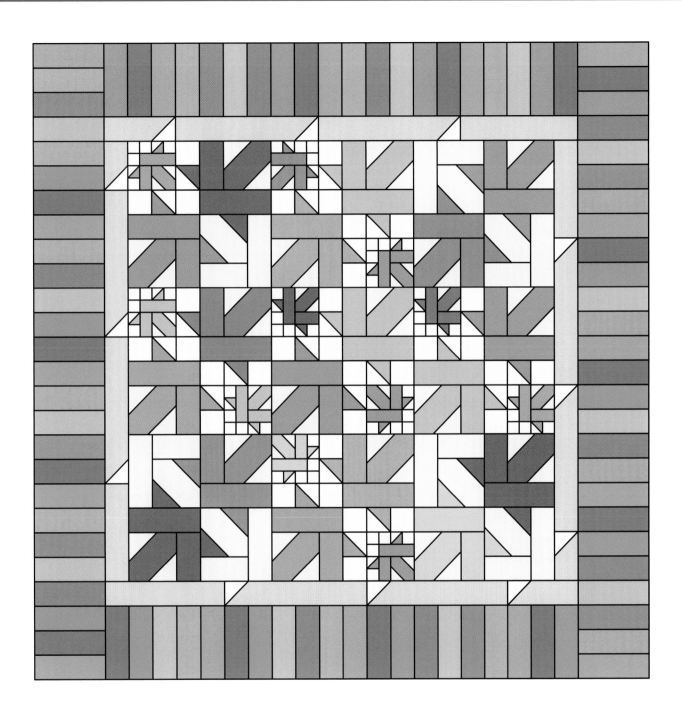

BUNKHOUSE SCRAPS

Finished Feathered Patchwork strip width: 1½"
Finished quilt top: 86" x 110"

Antique woven rugs, similar to BUNKHOUSE SCRAPS, are called "eye-dazzlers" or "Germantown" after the bright worsted wool from which they were made in the early American West. This quilt reflects the same grand tradition in the form of a quilt. Its reproduction-style prints and colors are reminiscent of the turn of the nineteenth century.

Fabrics and Supplies

- 2½ yards assorted light and medium print fabrics for Feathered Patchwork strips
- 3½ yards assorted dark print fabrics for Feathered Patchwork strips
- 2¼ yards of one medium blue print fabric for end wedges, side strips, and triangles
- ½ yard of light print fabric for pieced border
- 1 yard assorted bright and dark print fabrics for pieced border
- 2½ yards of one dark blue print fabric for outer border and binding
- 7¾ yards of fabric for backing (or 3¼ yards of 90"-wide fabric)
- 90" x 114" piece of batting

Cutting Fabrics

FEATHERED PATCHWORK STRIPS

From the light and medium print:
- Cut 14 strips, each 6" x 42". From these strips, cut 84 triangles.

From the assorted dark print:
- Cut 19 strips, each 6" x 42". From these strips, cut 112 triangles.

From the medium blue print:
- Cut three strips, each 6" x 42". From these strips, cut 14 triangles.
- Cut six strips, each 6" x 42". From these strips, cut 14 pairs of end wedges.

PIECED BORDER

From the light print:
- Cut 112 squares, each 2⅝" x 2⅝".

From the bright and dark print:
- Cut 15 strips, each 2¾" x 42". From these strips, cut 224 squares, each 2¾" x 2¾". Cut these squares diagonally for a total of 448 triangles.

OUTER BORDER AND BINDING

From the dark blue print:
- Cut nine strips, each 6" x 42".
- Cut twelve 2½" x 42" binding strips.

Cutting the End Wedges and Triangles

1. Fold the medium blue print strips in half and use the following dimensions to cut the 14 pairs of end wedges. Cut two end wedges at a time on each folded strip, and open up the fabric to cut one more end wedge from each strip.

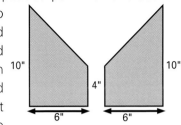

2. To cut the triangles from the assorted light, medium, and dark print fabrics, place a 6" x 24" acrylic ruler on the strip, aligning the 45° angle line with the edge of the strip. Make the first cut. Then rotate the ruler, so that you can repeat the process to cut the other side of the triangle. Take care to cut each triangle accurately.

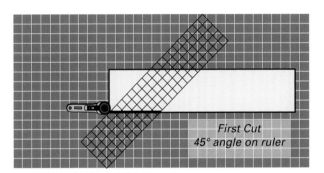

First Cut
45° angle on ruler

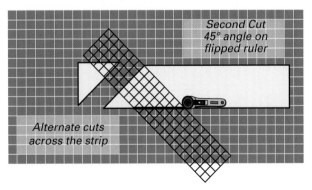

Second Cut
45° angle on flipped ruler

Alternate cuts across the strip

3. To ensure piecing accuracy, use a pencil to mark the center point of every light, medium, and dark triangle, so it will be easy to align the triangles correctly as you piece each Feathered Patchwork strip.

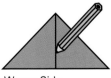

Wrong Side

Piecing Feathered Patchwork Strips

4. Sew a dark triangle to a medium end wedge, offsetting the triangle as shown, so that the edge of the triangle will be in correct alignment with the edge of the end wedge. Press the seam allowance toward the darker fabric each time you add another triangle. It is helpful to try out this technique using scrap fabrics, before piecing the Feathered Patchwork strips for the quilt center.

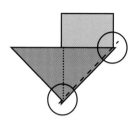

5. As you continue adding light or medium and dark triangles to the Feathered Patchwork strip, there will be a ¼" seam allowance at the tip of each triangle.

6. Sew together two 3½" x 42" medium blue print strips together to create an end strip. Press. Make one more end strip like this one. Lay out 14 Feathered Patchwork strips consisting of eight dark triangles and seven light or medium triangles, and two end wedges as shown below. Sew each of the strips together, as shown at right in the dia-

gram. Press each Feathered Patchwork strip.

7. Carefully cut Feathered Patchwork strip #1 into 2"-wide segments. Rearrange these strips and sew them together, as shown at top right, to create the first Feathered Patchwork strip.

8. Sew a 3½"-wide pieced medium blue print strip

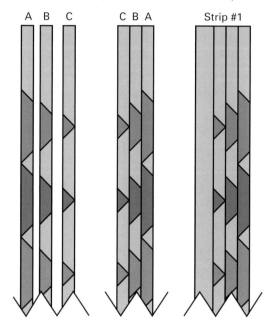

to the left side of Feathered Patchwork strip #1.

9. Repeat Steps 7 and 8 to cut and re-sew Feathered Patchwork strips #2 through # 7, referring to the diagram in Step 8. Sew Feathered Patchwork strip #8 together as a mirror image of Feathered Patchwork strip #1, referring to Step 7.

10. Sew the eight Feathered Patchwork strips together and press all seam allowances open.

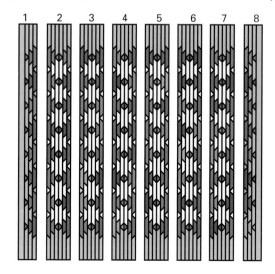

Trim the top and bottom edges of the quilt center so that it measures 93½" long.

Adding the Pieced Border

11. Sew four bright or dark triangles to each 2⅜" light square. Make a total of 112 of these units.

Make 112 units

12. Sew 31 Step 11 units together for each side of the quilt. Press the seam allowances open and sew these pieced units to the sides of the quilt center. Sew 25 Step 11 units together for the top and bottom edges of the quilt

center and press the seam allowances open. Sew these pieced units to the top and bottom edges of the quilt. Refer to the Quilt Assembly diagram above.

Adding the Outer Border

13. Sew remaining 42" dark blue print border strips together and press the seam allowance open. Repeat to make another border strip like this one. Measure your quilt to determine the correct length for the top, bottom, and side border strips. Cut the pieced strips to these lengths and sew them to the quilt, referring to the diagram above. Press the seam allowances toward the borders.

Finishing

15. Place the quilt backing wrong side up on a flat surface. Add the batting and the completed quilt top. Baste the three layers together.

FEATHERED CLOUDS & FLYING GEESE

Finished center panel strip width: 1½"
Finished quilt top: 52" x 64"

The light-colored Feathered Cloud blocks draw attention to the central portion of this design first, and the light areas of the Flying Geese border draw your eye outward toward the border. The play of color is secondary to the importance of light and dark values. Before you cut fabric for your quilt, consider doing a paste-up version using small scraps of fabric, or draw the quilt on graph paper and experiment with color combinations to determine what you like best.

Fabrics and Supplies

- 2 yards light tone-on-tone fabric for pieced center panel
- 1¾ yards dark print fabric for end wedges, outer border, and binding (save scraps for Flying Geese border)
- ¼ yard each of 8 coordinating medium to dark print fabrics for pieced center panel
- ⅞ yard total of assorted medium-to-dark print scraps for Flying Geese border
- 3¼ yards of fabric for backing (or 2 yards of 60"-wide fabric)
- 56" x 68" piece of batting

Cutting Fabrics

PIECED CENTER PANEL

From each 8 coordinating medium/dark:
- Cut a 6" x 42" strip. From this strip, cut two triangles.
- Cut five 6" x 42" strips. From each of these strips, cut six triangles. Reserve scraps for Flying Geese Border.

From the dark print:
- Cut five 6" x 42" strips. From one strip, cut four triangles. From the remaining four strips, cut ten mirror-image pairs of end wedges. Reserve scraps for Flying Geese Border.
- Cut two 3½" x 42" strips.

FLYING GEESE BORDER

From the medium/dark print fabrics and dark print scraps:
- Cut 128 rectangles, each 2" x 3½".

From the light tone-on-tone:
- Cut thirteen 2" x 42" strips. From these strips, cut 256 squares, each 2" x 2".

OUTER BORDER AND BINDING

From the dark print:
- Cut six 4" x 42" strips.
- Cut six 2½" x 42" binding strips.

Cutting the Triangles and Wedges

1. To cut the triangles from the light tone-on-tone fabric and the medium and dark print fabrics, place a 6" x 24" acrylic ruler on the strip, aligning the 45° angle line with the edge of the strip. Make the first cut. Then rotate the ruler, so that you can repeat the process to cut the other side of the triangle. Take care to cut each triangle accurately.

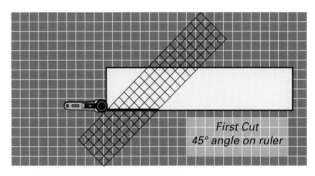

First Cut
45° angle on ruler

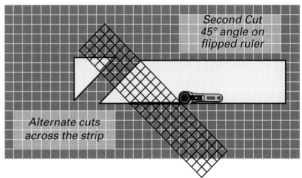

Second Cut
45° angle on flipped ruler

Alternate cuts across the strip

2. Fold the dark print strips in half and use the following dimensions to cut the 10 mirror-image pairs of end wedges. Cut two end wedges at a time on each folded strip, and open up the fabric to cut one more end wedge from each strip.

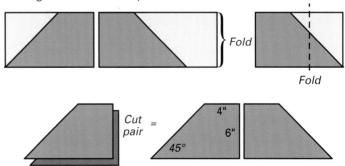

Fold

Fold

Cut pair =

4"

6"

45°

3. To ensure piecing accuracy, use a pencil to mark the center point of every light, medium, and dark triangle,

so it will be easy to align the triangles correctly as you piece each feathered patchwork strip.

Wrong side

Piecing the Center Panel

4. Lay out three light tone-on-tone triangles, two dark print triangles, and two dark print end wedges for the top section of the center panel, and sew them together, offsetting the pieces to make sure that the edges of the pieced strip will be straight, with ¼" seam allowances at the tips of the triangles. For offset diagram, see step 4, page 57. Press.

5. Cut the Step 4 panel into three 2"-wide strips.

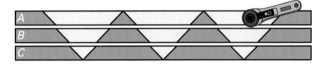

6. Rearrange the Step 5 strips into the "feathered" pattern, as shown, and sew them together. Press.

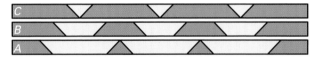

7. In the same manner, sew together the dark print end wedges. the coordinating dark print triangles, and light tone-on-tone print triangles for the next two sections of the center panel. Press. Cut each of these sections into three 2"-wide strips.

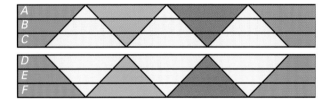

8. Pin the Step 7 strips together at the pencil marks for accuracy, and sew them together. Press. Sew the top section to the two Step 7 sections. Press.

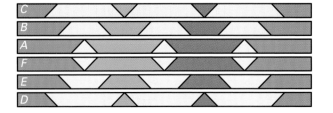

9. Referring to the diagram for color placements, repeat Step 7 to make six more pieced sections and the bottom pieced section. Press. Sew the pieced sections together to complete the center panel of the quilt. Press. The completed quilt center should measure 39½" x 57½". If necessary, trim to these measurements.

10. Trim two 3½" x 42" dark print strips to 37½" long and sew one strip to the top edge and one to the bottom edge of the quilt center, referring to the previous diagram. Press.

Adding the Flying Geese Border

11. Place a light tone-on-tone 2" square at one end of a dark print or coordinating medium/dark print 2" x 3½" rectangle, and sew them together with a diagonal seam. Press and trim the excess fabric on the wrong side to a ¼" seam allowance.

12. Repeat Step 11 at the other end of the rectangle, completing a Flying Geese unit. Press and trim the seam allowance as before. Make a total of 128 Flying Geese units.

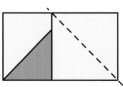
Seam allowance

Flying Geese Units, make 128

13. Sew two rows of 26 Flying Geese units each for the top and bottom Flying Geese Border strips, referring to the diagram on page 63. Sew these border strips to the top and bottom edges of the quilt center, referring to the Quilt Assembly diagram. Press the seam allowances toward the quilt center.

14. Sew two rows of 38 Flying Geese units each for the side Flying Geese Border strips, referring to Step 13. Sew these border strips to the sides of the quilt center (see diagram above) and press the seam allowances toward the quilt center.

Adding the Outer Border

15. Sew the six dark print 4" x 42" strips together and press the seam allowances open. Measure your quilt top from side to side through the middle to determine the correct measurement for the top and bottom outer border strips. Cut two dark print strips to this length and sew them to the top and bottom edges of the quilt, referring to the diagram above. Press.

16. Measure your quilt top vertically through the middle to determine the correct measurement for the side outer border strips. Cut two dark print strips to this length and sew them to the sides of the quilt, referring to the diagram above. Press.

Finishing

17. Place the quilt backing wrong side up on a flat surface. Add the batting and the completed quilt top. Baste the three layers together.

18. Quilt as desired, by hand or machine.

19. Apply the binding to the edges of the quilt.

GRETCHEN'S TRUMPET VINE

Finished blocks: 4½" square
Finished quilt top: 54½" x 72½"

Any type of fabric or scale of print will work well in these small Gretchen Blocks which makes them great for a scrap quilt. Light, medium, and dark values lend definition to the pieced blocks, and the medium-value appliqués stand out against the light fabric in the appliqué border. A very dark final border adds the perfect finishing touch.

Fabrics and Supplies

• 2½ yards total assorted light scrap fabrics for Gretchen Blocks, Sawtooth borders, and appliqué border
• 2½ yards total assorted medium to dark scrap fabrics for Gretchen Blocks, Sawtooth borders, and appliqué border
• 1 yard light fabric for background of appliqué border
• 1 yard dark fabric for outer border and binding
• 3½ yards of fabric for backing (or 2¼ yards of 60"-wide fabric)
58" x 76" piece of batting

Cutting Fabrics

GRETCHEN BLOCKS

From the light scrap:
• Cut five 3⅞" x 42" strips. From these strips, cut forty-eight 3⅞" x 3⅞" squares. Cut these squares in half diagonally.
• Cut fourteen 1⅝" x 42" strips. From these strips, cut ninety-six 1⅝" x 5½" rectangles.
• Cut six 2⅜" x 42" strips. From these strips, cut ninety-six 2⅜" x 2⅜" squares. Cut these squares in half diagonally.

From the medium to dark scrap:
• Cut five 3⅞" x 42" strips. From these strips, cut forty-eight 3⅞" x 3⅞" squares. Cut these squares in half diagonally.
• Cut fourteen 1⅝" x 42" strips. From these strips, cut 96 1⅝" x 5½" rectangles.
• Cut six 2⅜" x 42" strips. From these strips, cut ninety-six 2⅜" x 2⅜" squares. Cut these squares in half diagonally.

INNER SAWTOOTH BORDER

From the light scrap:
• Cut four 2⅜" x 42" strips. From these strips, cut sixty 2⅜" x 2⅜" squares. Cut these squares in half diagonally.
• Cut a 2" x 42" strip. From this strip, cut four 2" x 2" squares.

From the medium to dark scrap:
• Cut four 2⅜" x 42" strips. From these strips, cut 60 2⅜" x 2⅜" squares. Cut these squares in half diagonally.

APPLIQUÉ BORDER

TEMPLATES ON PAGE 69
From a light:
• Cut six 5" x 42" strips.

From the medium value scrap:
• Cut two and two reversed Birds.
• Cut 14 Trumpet Flowers.
• Cut 16 Trumpet Flower Buds.
• Cut 50 – 60 large and small leaves.
• Cut enough two 2"-wide bias strips across the width of one fabric to equal 100" of green vine.

OUTER SAWTOOTH BORDER

From the light scrap:
• Cut five 2⅜" x 42" strips. From these strips, cut 76 2⅜" x 2⅜" squares.

From the medium to dark scrap:
• Cut five 2⅜" x 42" strips. From these strips, cut 76 2⅜" x 2⅜" squares.

FINAL BORDER AND BINDING

From a dark :
• Cut eight 2¼" x 42" strips.
• Cut seven 2½" x 42" binding strips.

Piecing the Gretchen Blocks

1. With right sides together, chain-piece the 96 large light triangles to the 96 medium 1⅝" x 5½" rectangles. In the same manner, chain-piece the 96 large medium triangles to the 96 light 1⅝" x 5½" rectangles. Cut the threads between these units and press the seam allowances toward the darker fabric.

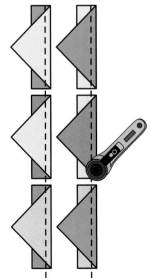

2. Align two small light triangles with each Step 1 unit featuring a medium rectangle. The edges of the small light triangles should be even with the edges of the large light triangle. Repeat this step, using two small medium triangles and the second group of Step 1 units.

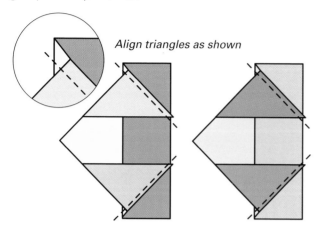

Align triangles as shown

3. Trim the excess fabric from the rectangles and press the seam allowances of the small triangles toward the darker fabric.

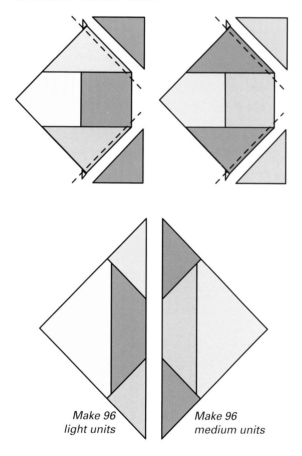

Make 96 light units

Make 96 medium units

4. You should have 96 units featuring a medium rectangle and 96 units featuring a light rectangle.

5. Place the two halves of each Gretchen Block side by side; one unit should have a large light triangle and one should have a large medium triangle. Pin the units together where the smaller triangles meet at the ¼" seam allowance and sew the two units together. Open the two units and press the center seam open. Make 96 Gretchen Blocks.

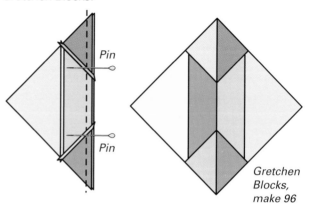

Pin

Pin

Gretchen Blocks, make 96

Assembling the Quilt Center

6. Sew 12 rows of eight Gretchen Blocks each. Press. Sew the 12 rows of blocks together, completing the quilt center. Press.

Adding the Inner Sawtooth Border

7. Sew 120 half-square triangle units, using the medium/dark and light triangles. Press. Sew two strips of 24 half-square triangle units each. Press. Sew the two strips with 24 half-square triangle units to the top and bottom edges of the quilt center. Press.

8. Referring to the diagram above, sew two strips of 35 half-square triangle units each. Sew a light 2" square to each end of these strips. Press. Sew these strips to the sides of the quilt center. Press.

Adding Appliqué, Outer Sawtooth Border, and Final Borders

9. Measure your quilt center from side to side through the middle to determine the correct length for the top and bottom appliqué border strips. Trim two 5" x 42" strips to this length and sew them to the top and bottom edges of the quilt center, referring to the Quilt Assembly diagram, page 68. Press.

10. Measure your quilt top vertically through the middle to determine the correct length for the side appliqué border strips. Sew two 5" x 42" light strips together, and press the seam allowance open. Trim this strip to the correct length, centering the seam. Repeat to make a second side appliqué border strip. Referring to the Quilt Assembly diagram, page 68, sew these border strips to the sides of the quilt center. Wait to add the appliqués until after the quilt top is completed.

11. Referring to Step 7, sew 152 half-square triangle units, using small light and medium/dark triangles.

12. Sew two Sawtooth border strips consisting of 32 half-square triangle units each. Press. Sew these border strips to the top and bottom edges of the quilt, referring to the Quilt Assembly diagram. Press.

13. Sew two Sawtooth border strips consisting of 44 half-square triangle units each. Add a 2" light square to both ends of these strips. Press. Referring to the Quilt Assembly diagram, sew these border strips to the sides of the quilt. Press.

14. Sew two 2¼" x 42" dark outer border strips together and press the seam allowance open. Repeat to make three more of these border strips.

15. Measure your quilt top from side to side through the middle to determine the correct length for the top and bottom outer border strips. Trim two dark outer border strips to this measurement, centering the seams, and sew them to the top and bottom edges of the quilt referring to the previous diagram. Press.

16. Measure your quilt top vertically through the middle to determine the correct length for the side outer border strips. Trim the remaining two dark outer border strips to this measurement, centering the seams, and sew them to the sides of the quilt referring to the previous diagram. Press.

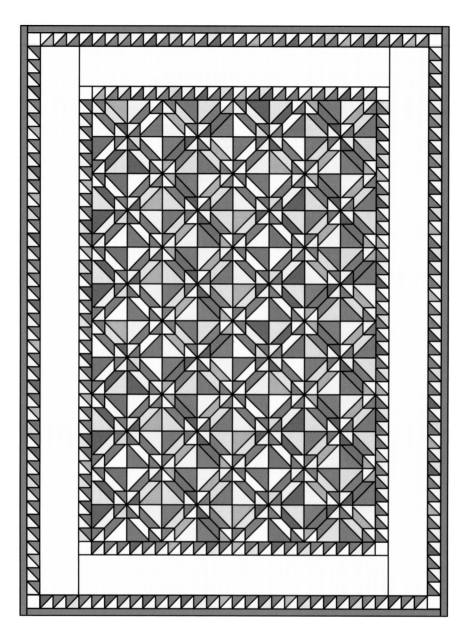

Adding the Appliqués

17. Prepare and cut the appliqué shapes for hand or machine appliqué, using the templates on page 69. Referring to the photo on page 64 for placement, stitch the vine first, and then add the Birds, Trumpet Flowers, Trumpet Flower Buds, and Leaves. If desired, use embroidery floss or perle cotton to add small decorative stitches to the Trumpet Flowers and Buds, referring to the templates for placements. Press the completed quilt top.

Finishing

18. Place the quilt backing wrong side up on a flat surface. Add the batting and the completed quilt top. Baste the three layers together.

19. Quilt as desired, by hand or machine.

20. Apply the binding to the edges of the quilt.

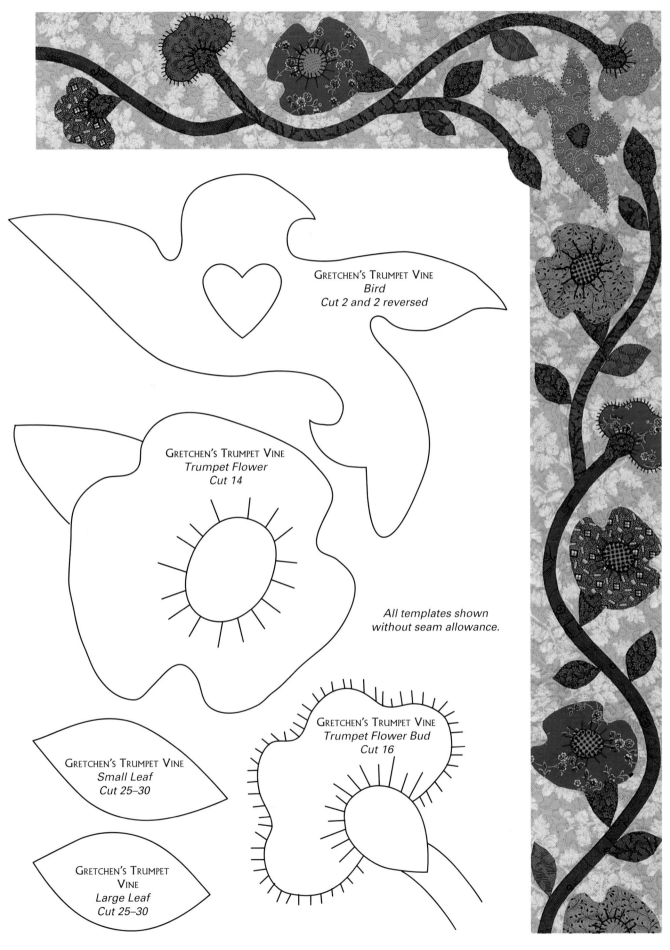

Gretchen's Trumpet Vine
Bird
Cut 2 and 2 reversed

Gretchen's Trumpet Vine
Trumpet Flower
Cut 14

All templates shown
without seam allowance.

Gretchen's Trumpet Vine
Small Leaf
Cut 25–30

Gretchen's Trumpet Vine
Trumpet Flower Bud
Cut 16

Gretchen's Trumpet
Vine
Large Leaf
Cut 25–30

ALMOST AMISH

Finished blocks: 6" square
Finished quilt top: 40" x 40"

Many Amish-style quilts are boldly graphic. They are the result of a very straightforward way of dealing with value and color contrast. Many modern quiltmakers and collectors are drawn to the contemporary look and calm elegance of older Amish quilts. The title of this quilt comes from the use of colors that would not likely be found in a traditional Amish quilt.

Fabrics and Supplies

- 1⅞ yards black solid fabric for Gretchen Blocks, borders, and binding
- 1 yard of scraps in assorted bright colors for Gretchen Blocks and borders
- 1½ yards of fabric for backing
- 44" x 44" piece of batting

Cutting Fabrics

GRETCHEN BLOCKS

From the black solid:

- Cut a 4⅞" x 42" strip. From this strip, cut eight 4⅞" x 4⅞" squares. Cut these squares in half diagonally.
- Cut two 2⅞" x 42" strips. From these strips, cut sixteen 2⅞" x 2⅞" squares. Cut these squares in half diagonally.
- Cut three 2" x 42" strips. From these strips, cut sixteen 2" x 6⅞" rectangles.

From the bright:

- Cut eight 4⅞" x 4⅞" squares. Cut these squares in half diagonally.
- Cut sixteen 2⅞" x 2⅞" squares. Cut these squares in half diagonally.
- Cut sixteen 2" x 6⅞" rectangles.

INNER SAWTOOTH BORDER

From the black solid:

- Cut two 2⅞" x 42" strips. From these strips, cut twenty-four 2⅞" x 2⅞" squares. Cut these squares in half diagonally.
- Cut a 2½" x 42" strip. From this strip, cut four 2½" x 2½" squares.

From the bright:

- Cut four 4½" x 42" strips.

OUTER SAWTOOTH BORDER AND BINDING

From the black solid:

- Cut two 2⅞" x 42" strips. From these strips, cut thirty-six 2⅞" x 2⅞" squares. Cut these squares in half diagonally.
- Cut a 2½" x 42" strip. From this strip, cut four 2½" squares.
- Cut five 2½" x 42" binding strips.

From the bright:

- Cut thirty-six 2⅞" x 2⅞" squares. Cut these squares in half diagonally.

Piecing the Gretchen Blocks

1. With right sides together, chain-piece the sixteen large bright triangles to the sixteen 2" x 6⅞" black rectangles. In the same manner, chain-piece the sixteen large black triangles to the sixteen 2" x 6⅞" bright rectangles. Cut the threads between these units and press the seam allowances toward the darker fabric.

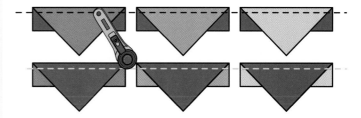

2. Align two small bright triangles with each Step 1 unit featuring a black rectangle. The edges of the small bright triangles should be even with the edges of the large bright triangle. Repeat this step, using two small black triangles and the second group of Step 1 units.

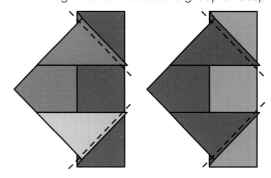

3. Trim the excess fabric from the rectangles and press the seam allowances of the small triangles toward the darker fabric. You should have sixteen units featuring a black rectangle and sixteen units featuring a bright rectangle.

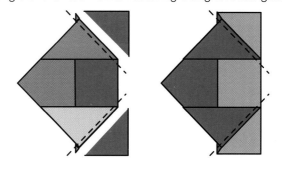

4. Place the two halves of each Gretchen Block side by side; one unit should have a large bright triangle and one with a large darker triangle.

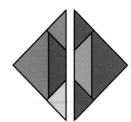

5. Pin the units together where the smaller triangles meet at the ¼" seam allowance and sew the two units together. Open the two units and press the center seam open. Make 16 Gretchen Blocks.

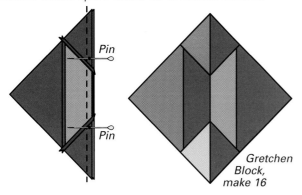

Gretchen Block, make 16

Assembling the Quilt Center

6. Sew four horizontal rows of four blocks each, alternating the diagonal seams of each block. Press.

7. Sew the four rows of blocks together to complete the quilt center. Press.

Adding the Inner Sawtooth Border

8. Sew 48 half-square triangle units, using the black and bright triangles. Press. Sew four strips of 12 half-square triangle units each. Press. Sew a 2½" black square at each end of two of these strips. Press. Sew the two strips with 12 half-square triangle units to the top and bottom edges of the quilt center. Press.

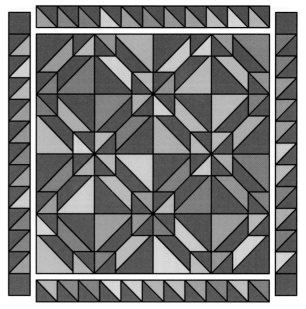

9. Sew the two strips with black squares to the sides of the quilt center. Press.

Adding the Middle Border

10. Measure your quilt top from side to side through the middle to determine the correct length for the top and bottom border strips. Trim two 4½" x 42" black strips to this measurement and sew them to the top and bottom edges of the quilt. Press.

11. Measure your quilt top vertically through the middle, including the border strips you just added. Trim two 4½" x 42" black border strips to this measurement. Referring to the diagram above, sew them to the sides of the quilt. Press.

Adding the Outer Sawtooth Border

12. Referring to Step 8, sew 68 half-square triangle units, using the black and bright triangles.

13. Referring to the diagram above, sew four strips of 18 half-square triangle units each. Press. Sew a 2½" black square at each end of two of these strips. Press. Sew the two strips with 18 half-square triangle units to the top and bottom edges of the quilt. Press. Sew the two strips with black squares to the sides of the quilt. Press.

Finishing

14. Place the quilt backing wrong side up on a flat surface. Add the batting and the completed quilt top. Baste the three layers together.

15. Quilt as desired, by hand or machine.

16. Apply the binding to the edges of the quilt.

MORRIS GARDEN

Finished blocks: 6" square
Finished quilt top: 60" x 60"

Bright red patchwork and appliqué tulips grace the five background fabrics in this heirloom quilt. The lightest background fabric occurs at the very center of the quilt, and the values of the others become slightly darker as they move toward the outer border and binding. The effect is like sunlight and shadows in a beautiful garden.

Fabrics and Supplies

- ⅓ yard light print fabric for background #1
- ¾ yard medium-light print fabric for background #2
- ½ yard medium print fabric for background #3
- ½ yard medium-dark fabric for background #4
- 2 yards dark fabric for background #5, outer border, and binding
- ½ yard assorted red print fabrics for tulips
- ⅛ yard black solid fabric for tulip centers
- ⅜ yard medium green print fabric for leaves
- 1 yard dark green print fabric for leaves and inner border
- ¼ yard light green print fabric for stems
- 3¾ yards of fabric for backing
- 64" x 64" piece of batting

Cutting Fabrics

BACKGROUNDS

From the light print fabric #1:
- Cut a 1¼" x 42" strip.
- Cut a 1½" x 42" strip. From this strip, cut eight squares, each 1½" x 1½".
- Cut two strips, each 2" x 42". From these strips, cut 24 squares, each 2" x 2".

From the medium-light print fabric #2:
- Cut two 1¼" x 42" strips.
- Cut two strips, each 1½" x 42". From these strips, cut 48 squares, each 1½" x 1½".
- Cut nine strips, each 2" x 42". From four of these strips, cut 64 squares, each 2" x 2".

From the medium print fabric #3:
- Cut two strips, each 5" x 42". From these strips, cut 16 squares, each 5" x 5".
- Cut three strips, each 2" x 42". From these strips, cut 48 squares, each 2" x 2".

From the medium-dark fabric #4:
- Cut two strips, each 6½" x 42". From these strips, cut 12 squares, each 6½" x 6½".

From the dark print fabric #5:
- Cut two strips, each 6½" x 42". From these strips, cut 12 squares, each 6½" x 6½".

TULIP BLOCKS

From the black solid:
- Cut a 1¼" x 42" strip.

From the assorted red print:
- Cut four strips, each 2" x 42".

LEAF BLOCKS

From the medium green print:
- Cut five strips, each 2" x 42".

From the dark green print:
- Cut four strips, each 2" x 42

INNER BORDER

From the dark green print:
- Cut eight strips, each 2" x 42".

OUTER BORDER AND BINDING

From the dark print fabric #5:
- Cut eight strips, each 5" x 42".
- Cut five 2½" x 42" binding strips.

APPLIQUÉ

TEMPLATES ON PAGES 79, 82, AND 83
From the assorted red print:
- Cut four large tulips.
- Cut four small tulips.

From the dark green print:
- Cut four leaves and four leaves reversed.

From the medium green print:
- Cut four leaf tips and four leaf tips reversed.

From the light green print:
- Cut eight 2" x 18" bias strips for stems.

Piecing the Tulip Blocks

1. Trim the 1¼" x 42" light print #1 strip and the 1¼" x 42" black solid strip to 8" long. Sew the 8"-long strips together and press the seam allowance toward the black fabric. Cut this strip set into four 1¼"-wide segments.

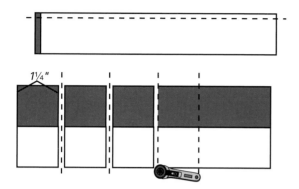

2 Sew the remaining portion of the black solid strip to a 1¼" x 42" medium-light print #2 strip and press the seam allowance toward the black fabric. Cut this strip set into 24 segments, each 1¼" wide.

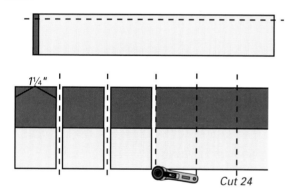

Cut 24

3. Sew the Step 1 units to the remaining portion of the 1¼"-wide light print #1 strip. Press. Cut the strip even with the edges of the Step 1 units.

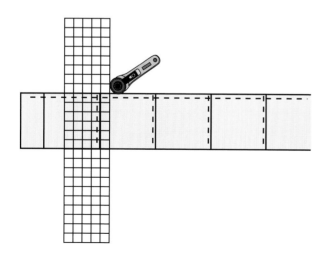

4. Sew the Step 2 units to a 1¼" medium light strip and press. Cut the strip even with the edges of the Step 2 units. Make four units with background fabric #1 and 24 units with background fabric #2.

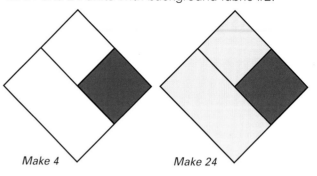

Make 4   Make 24

5. Sew the Step 3 and 4 units to 2" x 42" red strips. Press. Cut the red strips even with the edges of the Step 3 and Step 4 units.

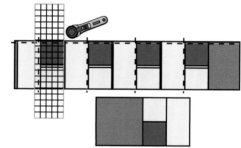

6. Sew the Step 5 units to 2" x 42" red strips. Cut the red strips even with the edges of these units.

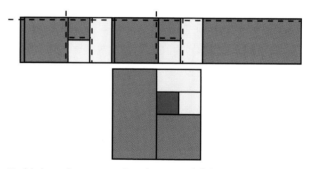

7. Using the same background fabric in each unit, sew two 1½" x 1½" squares to the Step 6 units with diagonal seams as shown. Open up the fabric and press. Trim the excess fabric on the wrong side of each unit to a ¼" seam allowance.

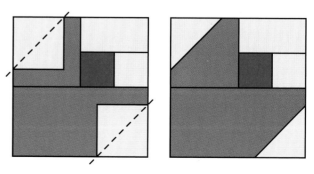

8. Sew the Step 7 units to a 2" x 42" strip of the appropriate background fabric. Trim the strip even with the edges of the Step 7 units. Sew these units to more 2" x 42" strips of the appropriate background fabric and trim the strips even with the edges of the units in the same manner.

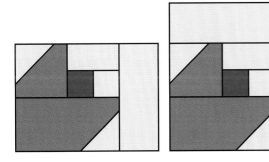

9. Referring to Step 8, add a 2"-wide green strip to each unit, followed by another green strip, referring to the diagram for color placements.

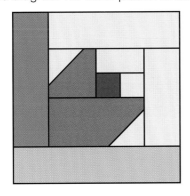

10. Referring to Step 7, sew two 2" x 2" squares to the Step 9 units with diagonal seams as shown. Take note of where each background color or green color is used. Open up the fabric and press. Trim the excess fabric on the wrong side of each unit to a ¼" seam allowance.

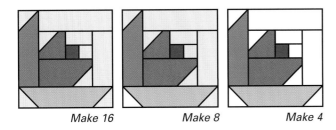

Make 16   Make 8   Make 4

Piecing the Leaf Blocks

11. Sew the sixteen 5" x 5" medium print background #3 squares to 2" x 42" dark green print strips. Cut the strips even with the edges of the squares and press the seam allowances toward the dark green print strips. In the same manner,

sew these units to 2" x 42" medium green print strips and cut the strips even with the edges of the units. Press the seam allowances toward the medium green print strips.

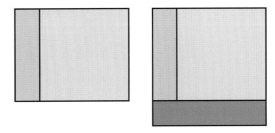

12. Sew a 2" x 2" background #3 square to each Step 11 unit with a diagonal seam as shown. Open up the fabric and press. Trim the excess fabric on the wrong side to a ¼" seam allowance.

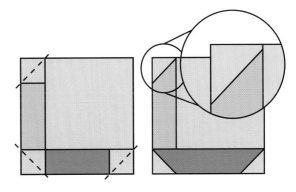

Assembling the Quilt Center

13. Arrange 24 Tulip blocks; 16 Leaf blocks; twelve 6½" x 6½" background #4 squares; and twelve 6½" x 6½" background #5 squares as shown below.

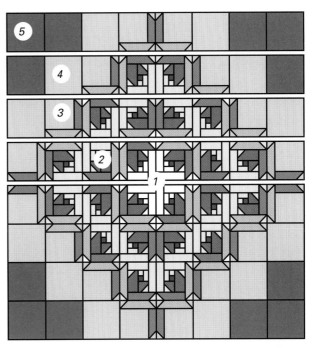

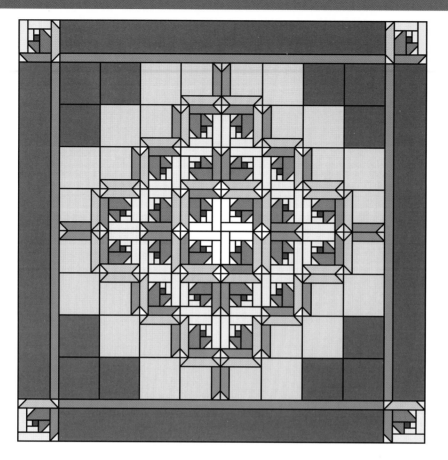

14. Referring to the previous diagram, sew the blocks into eight rows, pressing the seam allowances in opposite directions in alternating rows. Sew the rows of blocks together, completing the quilt center. Press.

Adding the Borders

15. Sew two 2" x 42" dark green strips together and press the seam allowance open. Make three more of these border strips. Sew two 5" x 42" dark print #5 strips together and press the seam allowance open. Make three more of these border strips. Sew a dark green pieced strip to a dark print #5 strip and press. Make three more of these pieced border strips.

16. Measure your quilt top both vertically and horizontally through the middle to determine the correct length for the pieced border strips. Trim four Step 15 strips to this length. Sew two of these strips to the top and bottom edges of the quilt center. Press the seam allowances toward the borders. Refer to the Quilt Assembly diagram above.

17. Sew a corner block to each end of the remaining two Step 15 strips, referring to the diagram above for placements. Press. Sew these borders to the side edges of the quilt. Press.

Adding the Appliqué

18. Referring to the photo on page 74 for placement, hand or machine appliqué two light green stems and two large leaves at each corner of the quilt center. Add a large and a small tulip to each stem.

19. In the same manner, hand or machine appliqué a light green stem and a large tulip on either side of each large leaf, allowing the tulips to extend into the middle of the outer border.

Finishing

20. Place the quilt backing wrong side up on a flat surface. Add the batting and the completed quilt top. Baste the three layers together. Quilt as desired, by hand or machine. Apply the binding to the edges of the quilt.

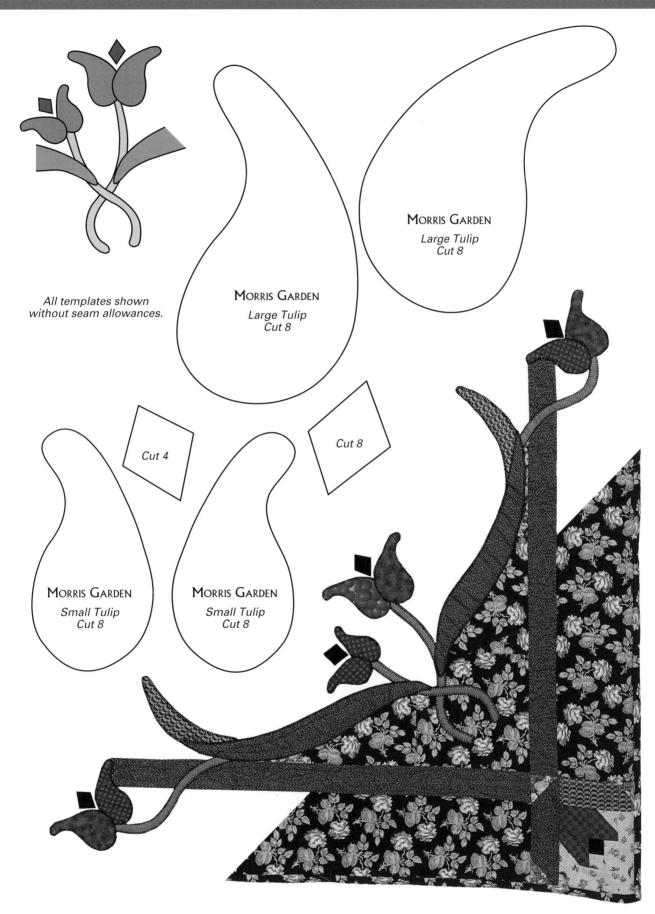

All templates shown
without seam allowances.

MORRIS GARDEN
Large Tulip
Cut 8

MORRIS GARDEN
Large Tulip
Cut 8

Cut 4

Cut 8

MORRIS GARDEN
Small Tulip
Cut 8

MORRIS GARDEN
Small Tulip
Cut 8

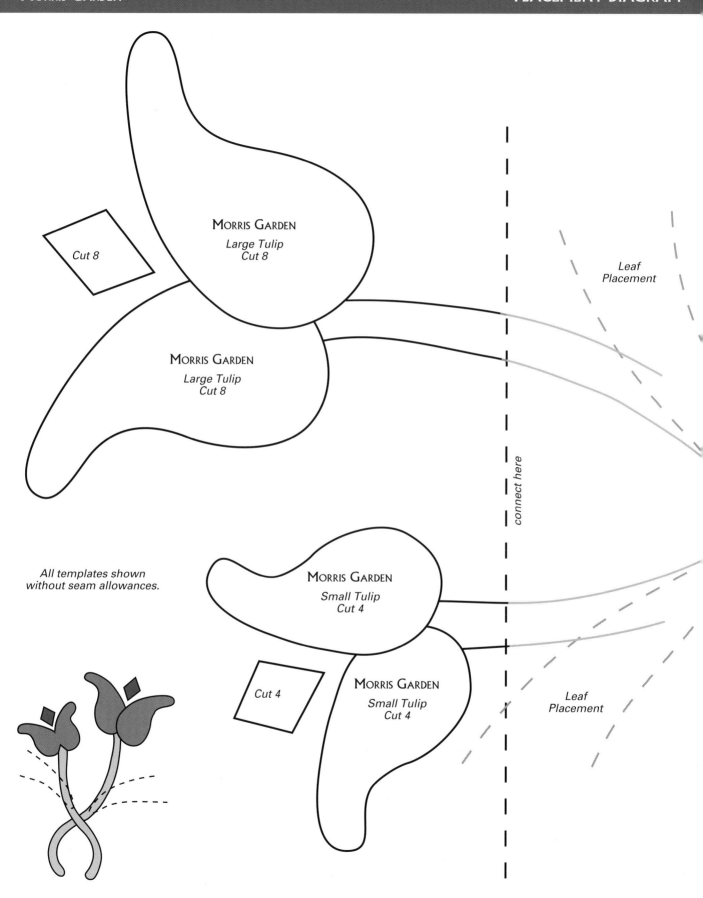

Cut 8

MORRIS GARDEN

*Large Tulip
Cut 8*

MORRIS GARDEN

*Large Tulip
Cut 8*

*Leaf
Placement*

connect here

*All templates shown
without seam allowances.*

MORRIS GARDEN

*Small Tulip
Cut 4*

Cut 4

MORRIS GARDEN

*Small Tulip
Cut 4*

*Leaf
Placement*

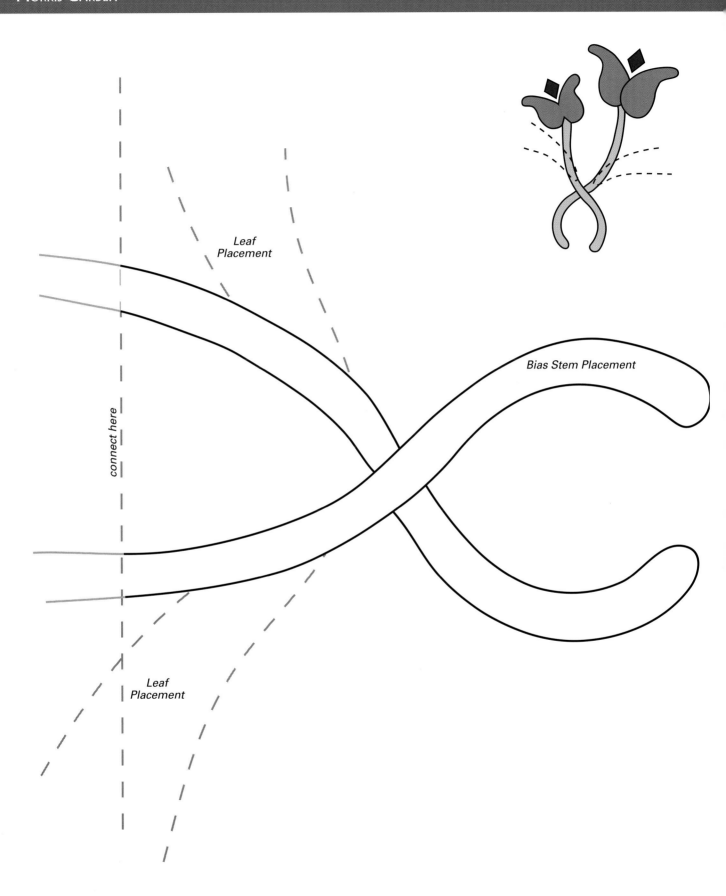

Leaf
Placement

Bias Stem Placement

connect here

Leaf
Placement

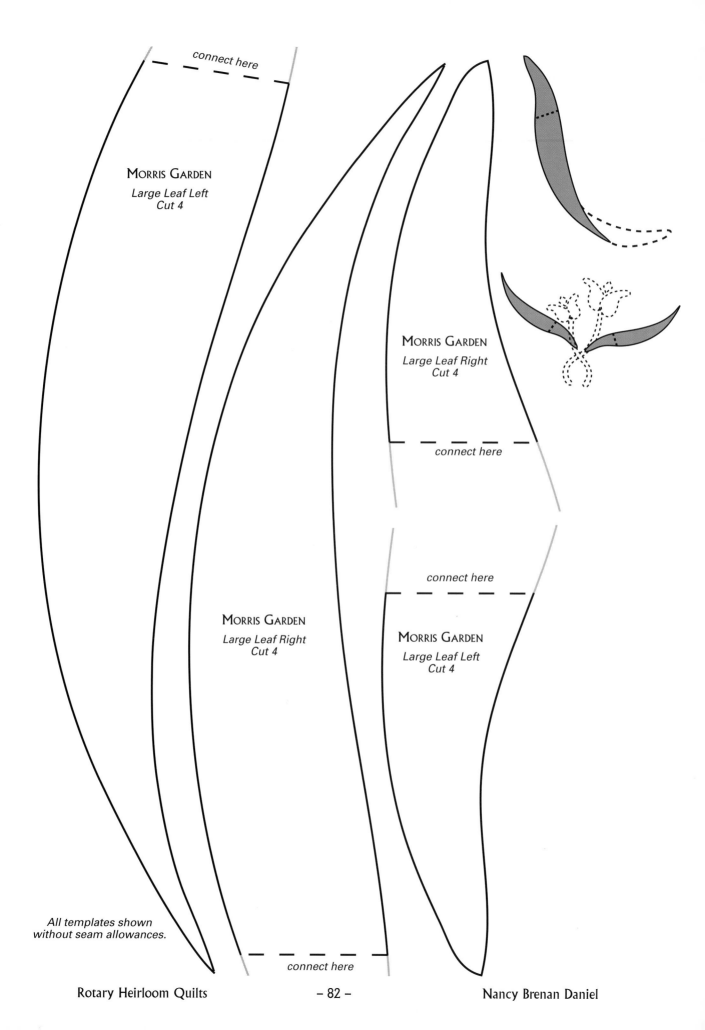

connect here

MORRIS GARDEN

*Large Leaf Left
Cut 4*

MORRIS GARDEN

*Large Leaf Right
Cut 4*

connect here

MORRIS GARDEN

*Large Leaf Right
Cut 4*

connect here

MORRIS GARDEN

*Large Leaf Left
Cut 4*

*All templates shown
without seam allowances.*

connect here

Rotary Heirloom Quilts
Nancy Brenan Daniel

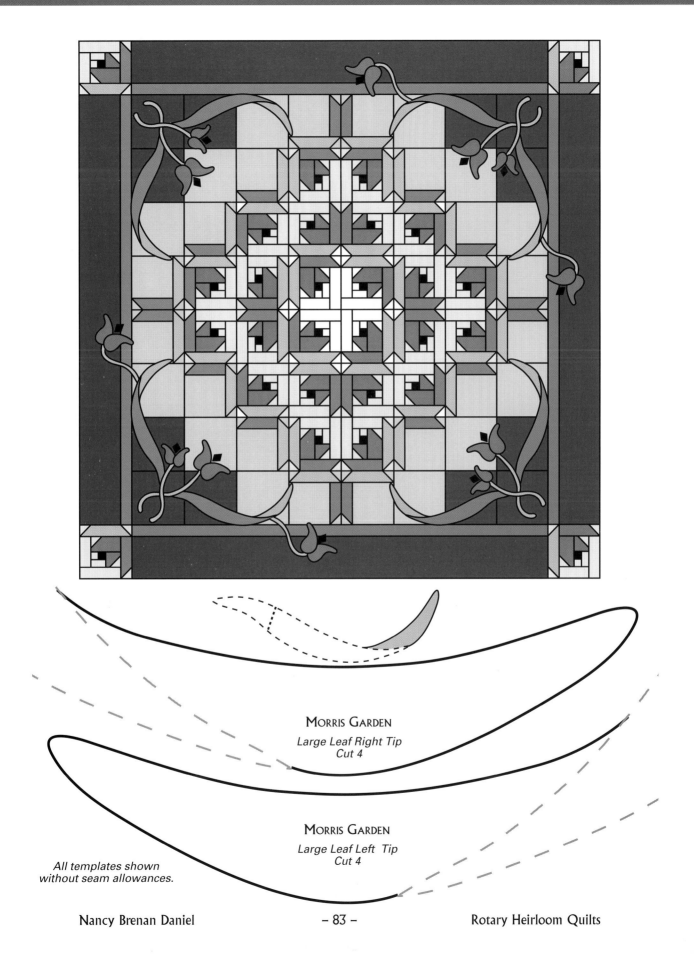

MORRIS GARDEN

*Large Leaf Right Tip
Cut 4*

MORRIS GARDEN

*Large Leaf Left Tip
Cut 4*

*All templates shown
without seam allowances.*

FOLKLORIC

Finished blocks: 24" square
Finished border units: 6" square
Finished quilt top: 71" x 71"

The four large Running-Feather blocks in this quilt are of my own invention.
An extra strip of the cheddar-colored background fabric around each block
makes the blocks appear to float on the background and opens up the center
area for the appliquéd flowers and leaves. The visual impact of this quilt
comes from the contrast between dull and bright fabrics and textures.

Fabrics and Supplies

- 3½ yards cheddar print for background
- 2 yards dark for one Running-Feather block, pieced and plain borders, and binding
- ⅓ yard each of three dark prints for three Running-Feather blocks
- ¼ yard each of two bright tone-on-tone yellow prints for Running-Feather blocks
- ¼ yard each of two bright tone-on-tone violet prints for Running-Feather blocks
- ¼ yard red print for flower appliqués
- ½ yard assorted green prints for stems and leaves
- ⅛ yard black print for flower centers
- ⅛ yard violet print for outer flower petals
- 3⅞ yards of fabric for backing (or 2 yards of 90"-wide fabric)
- 68" x 68" piece of batting

Cutting Fabric

RUNNING-FEATHER BLOCKS

From the cheddar print:
- Cut eleven strips, each 4½" x 42". From these strips, cut 48 mirror-image pairs of A wedges, template on page 92.
- Cut sixteen strips, each 1½" x 42". From these strips, cut eight strips, each 1½" x 24½" and eight strips, each 1½" x 26½".

From each dark print:
- Cut two strips, each 4½" x 42". From these strips, cut 16 mirror-image pairs of B wedges, template on page 92.

From each bright yellow and violet tone-on-tone:
- Cut a 4½" x 42" strip. From these strips cut four mirror-image pairs of A wedges of each, template on page 92.

From the assorted dark print fabrics:
- Cut seven strips, each 4½" x 42". From these strips, cut 64 mirror-image pairs of B edges, template on page 92.

From the yellow tone-on-tone print:
- Cut two strips, each 4½" x 42". From these strips, cut 8 mirror-image pairs of A wedges, template on page 92.

From the violet tone-on-tone print:
- Cut a 4½" x 42" strip. From these strips, cut 4 mirror-image pairs of A wedges, template on page 92.

BORDER AND BINDING

From the cheddar print:
- Cut eight strips, each 4½" x 42". From these strips, cut 32 mirror-image pairs of A wedges, template on page 92.
- Cut three strips, each 1½" x 42". From these strips, cut 16 mirror-image pairs of D wedges, template on page 93.
- Cut a 5¾" x 42" strip. From this strip, cut four 5¾" x 5¾" squares.

From the border dark print:
- Cut four strips, each 4½" x 42". From these strips, cut 32 mirror-image pairs of E wedges, template on page 93.
- Cut a 1½" x 42" strip. From this strip, cut 16 mirror-image pairs of E wedges, template on page 93.
- Cut a 6½" x 42" strip. From this strip, cut four C corner pieces, template on page 93.
- Cut six 4" x 42" outer border strips.
- Cut seven 2½" x 42" binding strips.

APPLIQUÉ

Templates on page 91
From the red print:
- Cut five flower shapes.

From the assorted green print:
- Cut four 2" x 15" bias strips for stems.
- Cut 16 small leaves.
- Cut eight large leaves.

From the black print:
- Cut five flower centers.

From the violet print:
- Cut 20 outer petals.

Cutting Wedges and Corner Pieces

1. To cut the A wedges for the Running-Feather Blocks and border, fold each 4½"-wide strip of fabric in half. Referring to the dimensions on the diagram, cut mirror-image pairs of wedges, aligning the 60° line on a ruler with the lower edge of the strip to cut the angled edges. You can cut four mirror-image pairs plus 1 more A piece from each folded strip.

A Wedge

2. To cut the B wedges for the Running-Feather Blocks and border, fold each 4½"-wide strip of fabric in half. Referring to the dimensions on the diagram, cut mirror-image pairs of wedges, aligning the 60° line on a ruler with the lower edge of the strip to cut the angled edges. You can cut 10 mirror image pairs from each folded strip.

B Wedge

3. To cut the C corner pieces for the pieced border, refer to the diagram and cut four pieces, aligning the 45° angle line on a ruler with the lower edge of the strip to cut the angled edges.

C Corner Piece

4. To cut the D wedges for the extra strips in the pieced border, fold each strip of fabric in half. Referring to the diagram, cut 16 mirror-image pairs of wedges, aligning the 60° angle line on a ruler with the lower edge of the cut strip to cut the angled edges. You can cut three mirror-image pairs from one strip.

D Wedge

5. To cut the E wedges for the extra strips in the pieced border, fold a strip of fabric in half. Referring to the diagram, cut 16 mirror-image pairs of wedges, aligning the 60° angle line on a ruler with the lower edge of the cut strip to cut the angled edges

E Wedge

Piecing Running-Feather Blocks

6. Match the dark print B wedges with the cheddar print A wedges, as shown. For the four Running-Feather blocks, you will need a total of 48 mirror-image pairs of A and B wedges. Sew the cheddar print A wedges to the dark print B wedges, offsetting the seam allowances as shown, so that the edges of the pieced strips will be straight. Press all seam allowances toward the dark B wedges.

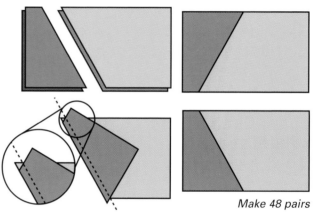

Make 48 pairs

7. Lay out two mirror-image Step 2 units. Cut each of these units into three 1½"-wide segments as shown.

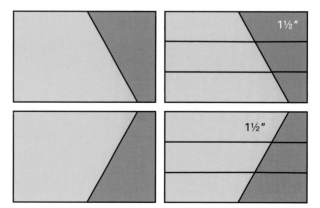

8. Rearrange the segments and sew them back together in the order shown. Press.

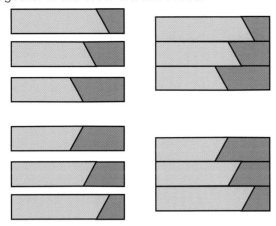

9. Trim the Step 8 units to 6½" square. Press. Make a total of 64 of these units in the following color combinations: four units with each yellow; four units with each violet; and 48 units with cheddar background fabric as shown. All of the units feature a different dark fabric.

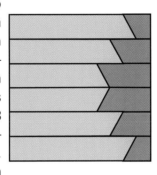

Make 64

10. Sew together three Step 9 units featuring cheddar and one unit featuring either yellow or violet, as shown. Press. Referring to the quilt photo on page 84 for color placements, sew together four of these units for each of the different color combinations.

Make 4

11. Lay out three Step 5 units and one Step 6 unit for one-quarter of each Running-Feather block. Sew the units together in pairs, and press. Sew the pairs of units together and press. Make four of these sections in each color combination. Sew the Running-Feather blocks together, so that the yellow or violet print areas form the center of each block. Press.

12. Sew a 1½" x 24½" cheddar print strip to opposite edges of each Running-Feather block. Press. Sew a 1½" x 26½" cheddar print strip to the remaining edges of each block. Press.

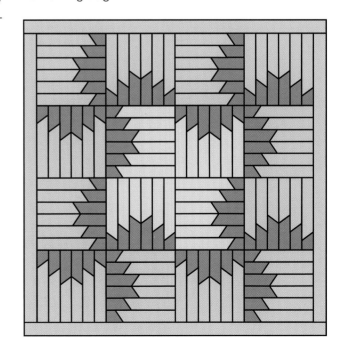

Assembling the Quilt Center

Referring to the Quilt Assembly diagram, sew the Running-Feather Blocks together in pairs and press. Sew the pairs of blocks together and press.

Adding the Border Units

13. Sew a cheddar print D wedge to a dark print E wedge, offsetting the seam allowances in the same manner as for the A and B wedges. Press. Make a total of 16 of these "extra" units to fill in the middle and end of each border.

Make 16

14. Sew a dark print C corner piece to a cheddar print triangle and press. Make a total of four of these corner units.

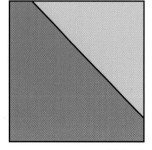

Make 4

Corner Unit

15. To sew the border units, refer to "Piecing Running-Feather Blocks" on page 86. Each of the four border units consists of eight pairs of A/B wedges cut and re-sewn together, with two Step 13 units between them, and a Step 13 unit at each end. Press the completed border units.

16. Sew two Step 15 border units to the sides of the quilt top and press. Sew a Step 14 corner unit to each end of the remaining two border units and press. Sew these borders to the remaining sides of the quilt, referring to the diagram. Press.

Adding the Outer Border

17. Measure your quilt to determine the correct measurement for the top and bottom outer border strips. Sew four pairs of 4" x 42" dark print strips together and press the seam allowances open. Repeat. Trim two of these border strips to the correct length and sew them to the top and bottom edges of the quilt top, see the previous diagram. Press the seam allowances toward the borders.

18. Measure your quilt top vertically through the middle to determine the correct measurement for the side outer border strips. Trim the remaining two border strips to this length and sew them to the sides of the quilt. Press the seam allowances toward the borders.

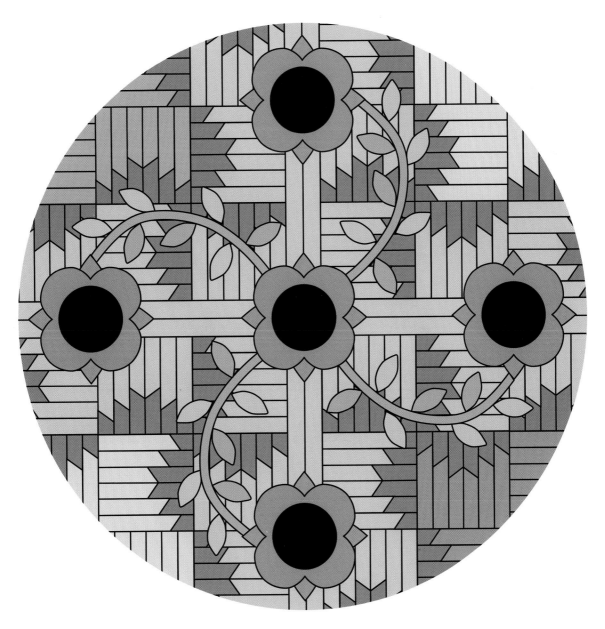

Adding the Appliqués

19. Trace the Flower, the Center Circle, the outer petal, and the small and large leaf shapes from page 91 onto template plastic and cut out each shape on the marked lines. Mark around each template on the right side of the appropriate fabric for each shape, and cut the number of each shape indicated, with a ¾₆" seam allowance.

20. Appliqué the stems in place, see the photo on page 84 for placement.

21. Pin four flowers in place at the end of each stem and one flower at the center of the quilt. Pin the outer petals in position underneath each flower. Appliqué the outer petals in place. Appliqué the flowers and center circles over the outer petals.

22. Appliqué the large and small leaves, referring to the photo on page 84 and illustration above for placements.

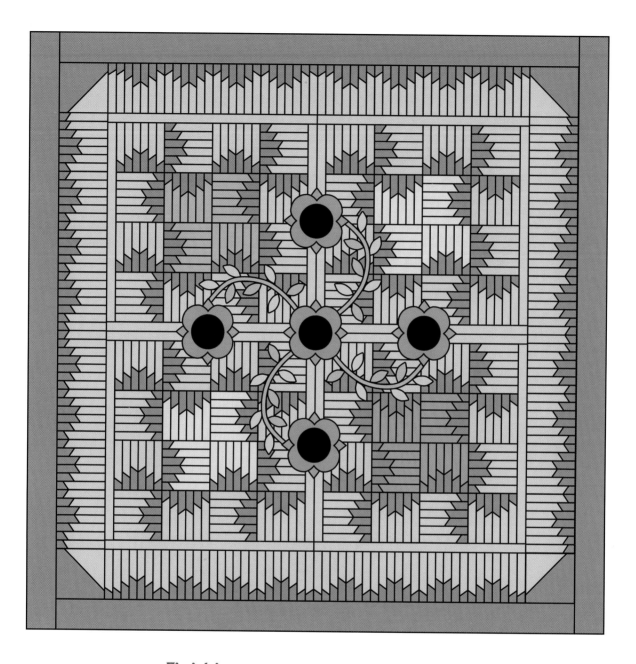

Finishing

23. Place the quilt backing wrong side up on a flat surface. Add the batting and the completed quilt top. Baste the three layers together.

24. Quilt as desired, by hand or machine.

25. Apply the binding to the edges of the quilt.

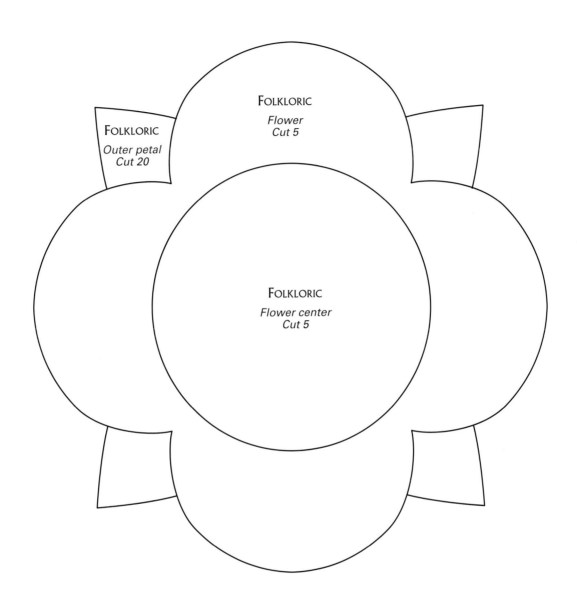

FOLKLORIC

Flower
Cut 5

FOLKLORIC

Outer petal
Cut 20

FOLKLORIC

Flower center
Cut 5

All templates shown
without seam allowances.

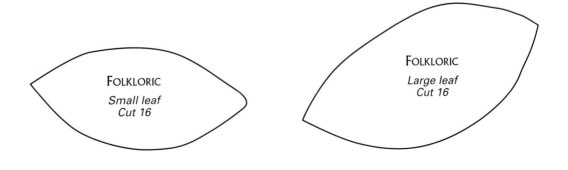

FOLKLORIC

Small leaf
Cut 16

FOLKLORIC

Large leaf
Cut 16

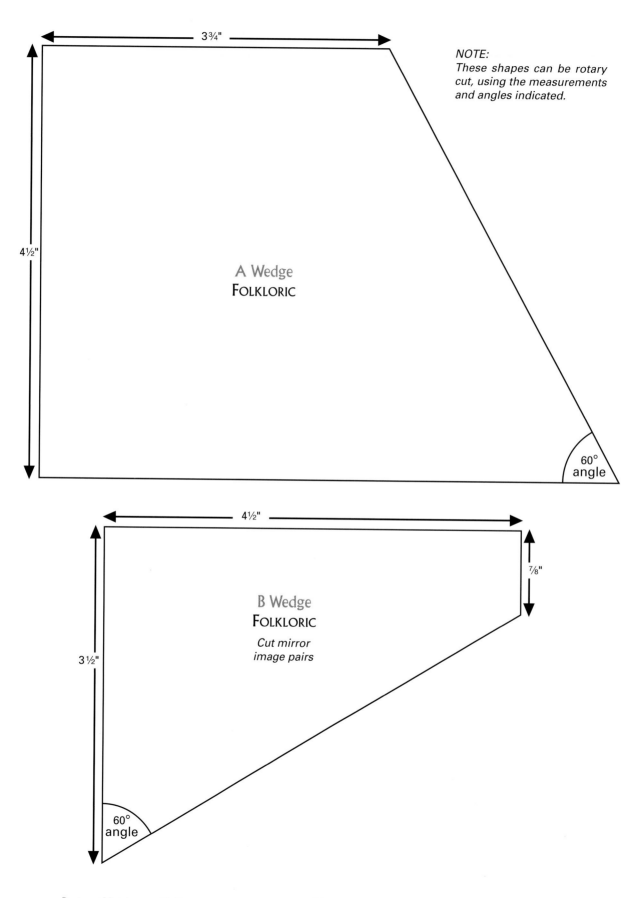

3¾"

NOTE:
These shapes can be rotary
cut, using the measurements
and angles indicated.

4½"

A Wedge
FOLKLORIC

60°
angle

4½"

⅞"

B Wedge
FOLKLORIC

Cut mirror
image pairs

3½"

60°
angle

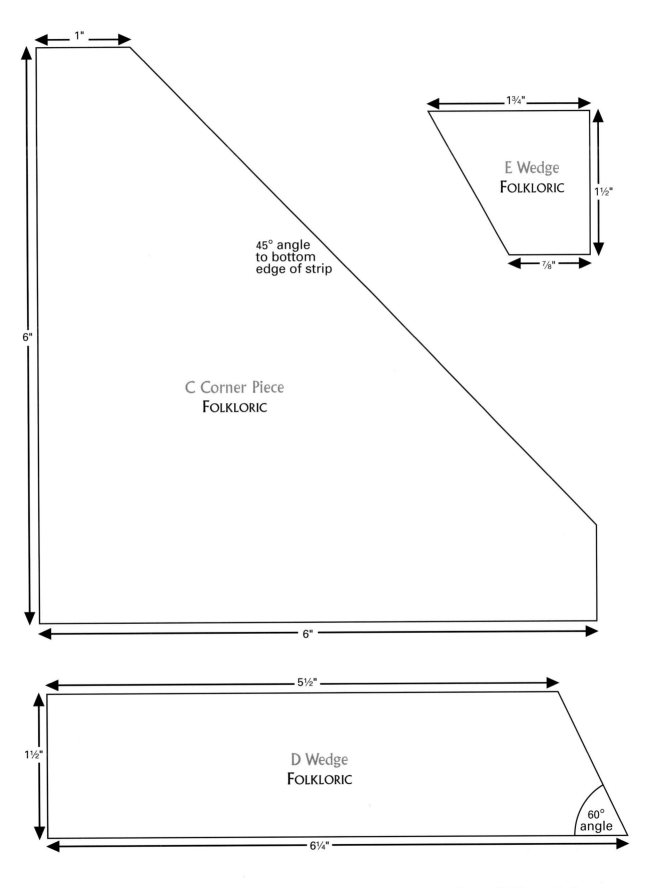

1"

6"

45° angle
to bottom
edge of strip

C Corner Piece
FOLKLORIC

6"

1¾"

E Wedge
FOLKLORIC

1½"

⅞"

5½"

1½"

D Wedge
FOLKLORIC

6¼"

60°
angle

BIBLIOGRAPHY

Bishop, Robert and Elizabeth Safanda. *A Gallery of Amish Quilts*. New York: E.P. Dutton, Inc., 1976.

Barnes, Christine. *Color: The Quilter's Guide*, That Patchwork Place, 1997.

Birren, Faber. *Principles of Color*, Schiffer, Inc., 1987.

Daniel, Nancy Brenan. *Learn How to Hand Quilt in Just One Day*, The American School of Needlework, 1996.

Daniel, Nancy Brenan. *Learn How to Appliqué*, The American School of Needlework, 1997.

Hallock, Anita. *A Treasury of Strip Quilt Projects*, Chilton Book Company, 1989.

Hargrave, Harriet. *Heirloom Machine Quilting*, C & T Publishing, 1995.

Itten, Johannes. *The Elements of Color*, Van Nostrand Reinhold, 1970.

Johannah, Barbara. *The Quick Quilting Handbook*, Pride of the Forest Press, 1979.

Johannah, Barbara. *Half-Square Triangles: Exploring Design*, Barbara Johannah, 1987.

Johannah, Barbara. *Crystal Piecing*, Chilton, 1993.

Leman, Bonnie. *Taking the Math Out of Making Patchwork Quilts*, Moon Over the Mountain Publishing, Co.,1981.

McCloskey, Marsha. *Quick Classic Quilts*, Oxmoor House, 1996.

Penders, Mary Coyne. *Color and Cloth*, The Quilt Digest Press, 1989.

Poster, Donna. *The Quilter's Guide to Rotary Cutting*, Chilton, 1991.

Perry, Gai. *Color from the Heart*, C & T Publishing, 1999.

Thomas, Donna Lynn. *Shortcuts: A Concise Guide to Rotary Cutting*, That Patchwork Place, 1991.

Townswick, Jane. *Artful Appliqué: The Easy Way*, That Patchwork Place, 2000.

ABOUT THE AUTHOR

Nancy Brenan Daniel has enjoyed quiltmaking all of her adult life. She learned to love and appreciate quilts from her grandmother, Mary Talkington Ritzenthaler, who encouraged her to play with fabrics and quilts at a very young age. In turn, Nancy has also encouraged her mother, Mary Ritzenthaler Brenan, to complete two quilts of her own.

Nancy has been an art educator for more than 30 years, teaching art history, color, and design. Although quiltmaking and design currently take up much of her time, she continues to volunteer at the Arizona State University Art Museum.

Active in the quilt world for many years as a popular teacher and designer, Nancy is the author of 18 books on sewing and quiltmaking and is a regular contributor to quilting magazines. Her quilt, ORIENTAL COOL, was the cover quilt for the AQS *Quilt Art 1986 Engagement Calendar*, and her RED AND WHITE GRETCHEN quilt was chosen as the cover quilt for the *2002 Better Homes and Gardens Engagement Calendar*. She is a certified teacher and judge of the National Quilting Association, Inc., and remains active in several local and national quilt guilds. She is a Charter Member of the American Quilter's Society and a member of the Museum of the American Quilter's Society.

OTHER AQS BOOKS

This is only a small selection of the books available from the American Quilter's Society. AQS books are known worldwide for timely topics, clear writing, beautiful color photos, and accurate illustrations and patterns. The following books are available from your local bookseller, quilt shop, or public library.

#6210   us$24.95

#5850   us$21.95

#5708   us$22.95

#5755   us$21.95

#6005   us$19.95

#5756   us$19.95

#5761   us$22.95

#4995   us$19.95

#6212   us$25.95

Look for these books nationally or call **1-800-626-5420**